2⁷⁵

The Full Knowledge of the Word of God

Witness Lee

Living Stream Ministry
Anaheim, California

First Edition, 6,250 copies. June 1987.

Library of Congress Catalog
Card Number: 87:81745

ISBN 0-87083-288-3 (hardcover)
ISBN 0-87083-289-1 (softcover)

Published by

Living Stream Ministry
1853 W. Ball Road, P. O. Box 2121
Anaheim, CA 92804 U.S.A.

Printed in the United States of America

CONTENTS

PREFACE

The messages contained in this book and in two related books entitled *Everyone Speaking the Word of God* and *Meeting to Speak the Word of God* were given in October, 1985 in Taipei, Taiwan during a training in which the author spoke three times daily. These messages have been translated from the Chinese.

CHAPTER ONE

THE ESSENCE OF GOD'S WORD

Scripture Reading: 1 Tim. 2:4; John 17:17; 2 Tim. 3:16; 1 Pet. 2:2; Matt. 4:4; John 6:63; 1:1, 14

OUTLINE

I. The essence of God's Word:
   A. The divine breath—2 Tim. 3:16.
   B. The spiritual milk—1 Pet. 2:2.
   C. The bread of life—Matt. 4:4.
   D. Spirit and life—John 6:63.
   E. Christ—God Himself—John 1:1, 14.

Beginning this morning we will have five days of training meetings on service. Every brother and sister in the church has a part. It is not only the elders and co-workers who serve, but every brother and sister in the church is a serving one.

Before the meeting you received the outline for this message. In the outline there are Scripture verses. Before I came downstairs, I told a few of the co-workers not to tell you how to read the verses because I wanted to see how you would do it. I watched carefully. Your prayers were quite good, but you prayed without stopping. I had no choice, so I asked someone to write two verses on the blackboard. Then he said, "Let us pray-read." After he said this, you began to pray-read. You should know that time is limited in a training; therefore, after you have prayed a little while, you should begin to pray-read.

EVERYONE BEING ABLE TO PRAY
AND TO READ IN THE MEETINGS

Whenever we gather together, we enter into the Lord's name. We have been called out of everything to be gathered together. The Spirit is within us, and the Word of the Lord is in our hands; therefore, we can read and we can pray. We do not have a pastor, and even though we have elders, they are not elders in the meetings. In the meetings, everyone is equal. We have many co-workers, but they are not co-workers in the meetings. Their work is to preach the gospel on the campuses, to lead people to be saved, to hold special meetings, and to take care of the saints in the church.

When the church gathers together, we all have the Word of the Lord, and we also have the Spirit of the Lord. We can use our eyes to read the Lord's Word, our mind to understand the Lord's Word, and our spirit to pray over and receive the Lord's Word. We all can do these things, just as everyone can breathe, drink, eat, and speak. We all are living people, not robots. The God whom we serve is also living. We are not serving dumb idols. When we come to the meetings, we desire to overturn the way of practice in Christianity, which stifles the functioning of the members of the Body of Christ. For several decades we have been trying to overturn this way, but sometimes the more we tried the more we fell back into it. When I came back to Taiwan in October 1984, I could not tolerate the situation any longer; I made up my mind to overturn all the things related to the old way. However, this morning these things are still with us. My reason for mentioning this to you is to ask you to overturn these old things.

GRASPING THE MAIN POINTS TO PRAY-READ

In addition, when you pray-read, you need to look at the subject and the main points. The subject this morning is "The Full Knowledge of the Word of God." Therefore, when you pray-read 1 Timothy 2:4, "Who desires all men to be saved and come to the full knowledge of the truth," you should not dwell on the phrase "who desires all men to be saved," because the subject is not salvation but knowing the truth. In this sense, pray-reading may be likened to playing basketball. In basketball the main thing is not dribbling but shooting. In pray-reading, when you "get the ball," do not dribble the ball; just shoot.

When I came back to Taiwan, I saw that all the industries on this island had changed and that the export business had been revolutionized. However, the way we do things has not changed much. We cannot change the earth, which was created by God, but we can change the method of transportation on the earth. Likewise, we cannot change the truth, but we can change our way of practicing the truth. Therefore, this training is not for a specific class of people but for everyone. From now on there will be no class in the service of the church. We must hate class structure, and we must abolish class structure. When the class structure is abolished, there will be no religious organization and no clergy.

HAVING GOD'S WORD
AND BEING ABLE TO SPEAK GOD'S WORD

Because of the change of the system, we have turned from big meetings to small meetings. In the small meetings our greatest need is the word of God. Everyone should know how to speak the word of God. A short time ago I was in a special conference in Berkeley, California. There I spoke five messages on "The Divine Speaking." In these messages I taught and encouraged the saints to speak the divine word. When I returned to Taiwan, this was still my burden. I feel that the small group meetings have not been firmly established and are not rich because we do not have enough of God's word, and we do not have sufficient experience in speaking God's word. Using again the illustration of basketball, we all know that having a basketball is one thing, and playing the game of basketball is another thing. If you do not have enough practice in the basic movements and have not practiced enough to work together with the other team members, you cannot play a good game. In like manner, to have God's word is one thing, and to speak God's word is another thing. I believe that many of you who are in the meetings have God's word, but because you lack practice in speaking, when you need to speak you cannot do it. These two matters—having God's word and speaking God's word—

are our present need. If we cannot master these two things, it will be difficult to succeed in changing the system.

I do not expect the changing of the system to succeed in six months, but I do expect that it will succeed in three years. Anything worthwhile cannot be done successfully in one try. Anything that can be done successfully in a short time is probably not very worthwhile. Therefore, we need to have patience and perseverance. We need to struggle, work hard, and practice; then we will succeed in changing the system. Therefore, having come back to Taiwan this time, I still need to emphasize these two points: having the word of God and speaking the word of God. Every day we will have three training meetings, two in the morning and one in the evening. The subject of the first message each day will be "The Full Knowledge of the Word of God," and the subject of the second message will be "Everyone Speaking the Word of God." In the first message the emphasis will be on the word, while in the second message the emphasis will be on speaking. The subject of the third message will be "Meeting to Speak the Word of God."

GOD DESIRING ALL MEN TO COME
TO THE FULL KNOWLEDGE OF THE TRUTH

I was raised in Christianity and participated in three denominations. I studied in a Baptist elementary school and also went to a Baptist Sunday School. Then I gained some further learning in the Chinese Christian Presbyterian Church. Later, I went to the Brethren Assembly to learn the truth in the Bible. At that time the Brethren Assembly was very famous in northern China. I attended their meetings five times a week, rain or shine, for seven and a half years. I heard many sermons, and in these sermons the phrase "God desires all men to be saved" was often repeated. However, I never heard anyone tell me that God not only desires all men to be saved, but He also desires all men to come to the full knowledge of the truth. In the Chinese Union Version, the translation of 1 Timothy 2:4 is, "Who will have all men to be saved and know the true principle." The "true principle" here is the truth. We cannot say that "know" is a wrong translation, but it does not bring out the full meaning. In the original text this word, *epignosis*, is derived from a verb, *epiginosko*. The prefix of this word, *epi*, means "exactly, completely, through and through." This word indicates not merely a little knowledge but a thorough and complete knowledge.

Many Christians pay attention only to "God desires all men to be saved" and neglect the other part of God's desire. After we are saved, whether or not we will be useful vessels in God's hand depends on our attitude toward the truth. If we know only a little of the truth, there will be a great lack. God surely desires all men to be saved, but He does not stop there. He also desires that all men come to the full knowledge of the truth. Not only in Christianity, but even among us, there are some who have been attending meetings for many years but who cannot give a complete message on any point of the truth. What a pity!

BEING ABLE TO APPREHEND THE TRUTH AND ALSO TO PUT IT INTO WORDS

When brothers and sisters stand up to speak in the meetings, we can discern from their speaking the measure of the truth that is in them. It is often possible to determine a person's educational level from his speaking. For example, even now I still recognize a few brothers and sisters who met with us in 1949. I am afraid that if you were to ask them to give a ten minute message on God's justification, they would not be able to do it. Everyone is able to stand up and give a testimony, but when we ask many of the saints to speak the truth, they are not able to do it. It is for this reason that we must change the system.

In the United States I told some people that, during the time from 1962 until today, a period of almost twenty-three years, their sons had graduated from college, but they, the parents, could not even give a message. In the spiritual sense, they had not even graduated from elementary school. This is where we have failed. Brothers and sisters, here in Taiwan we also have been meeting together for more than thirty years. How many of you can stand up and speak concisely, clearly, simply, understandably, and thoroughly for five to ten minutes? I doubt very much that I can find even one.

If we cannot speak spiritual words, how can we go out to supply life, release the truth, and preach the gospel? We will only be able to tell people, "It is very good to believe in Jesus. If you believe, you will have joy and peace; therefore, you must believe." If we need to speak further concerning the benefits of believing, we can only say, "Come and see. Come and listen, and you will know. You can only know these things by experience; I cannot tell you in words how good it is." If it cannot be put into words, how can I tell you about it, and how did you hear about it? The reason that you cannot put it into words is that you did not learn how to do it.

Many brothers and sisters in the United States were moved by the Lord and began to form gospel teams. Two or three teams began to go out to preach the gospel on many university campuses in many states. I had told them before that, even though the United States is a country of high education, the gospel that has been preached there is still elementary. It speaks either about going up to heaven, about going down to hell, or about peace and joy. But the truth in the Bible is high. Because of this, I told them that they should go out to preach the high gospel, the gospel that people cannot help but receive. However, they always had a question: "Do you think that people will understand these things that we speak?" In answer to this I said, "Do not say that people cannot understand. It is not that they cannot understand but that you do not know how to speak. If you can speak, they will understand." These words encouraged them. They formed gospel teams and preached the Triune God—the Father, the Son, and the Spirit—as the gospel. The result was wonderful. When they came back to give a report, they all were excited and said, "It is wonderful! The students on the university campuses welcomed this subject the most. One by one they were saved because of this subject."

How do you explain this? Therefore, we must change our concept.

PREACHING THE HIGH GOSPEL

Today the educational standard in Taiwan is high. If you preach the gospel only of going to heaven and not going to hell, people will not be interested. This kind of preaching can only frighten the very old and the very young. In this age you cannot preach this kind of low gospel. This does not mean that the Bible does not speak of heaven and hell, but that people today do not need this. They are thirsty for the high gospel. You must tell them that the Triune God entered into humanity, not only to be our Savior, but also to be our life, and even to become the meaning of our life. Anyone who is even a little philosophical in his thinking will welcome and receive this. Therefore, brothers and sisters, today if we do not have a considerable amount of education in the truth, our service cannot meet the demand of the present age. As a result of the diligent labor of the brothers, the number attending the Chinese-speaking meeting in Anaheim has increased. Among those who attend this meeting are some who have worked in the Chinese society. They are intellectual and philosophical people, and they are all over sixty years of age. When we speak to them about the gospel of life, they feel that it is very meaningful, and they are interested.

LABORING IN THE BIBLE

I hope that you can all see that this is a new age. We must change the system. It would be ridiculous if we still used an old oxcart to travel around the world. I thank the Lord that you all love the Lord. Some of you are even full-timers. Six months ago I charged you to spend four hours, from eight o'clock until noon, on Monday through Saturday mornings to study the Bible. In this message we have said that God desires all men not only to be saved but also to come to the full knowledge of the truth. What is the truth? The Word of God, the Bible, is the truth (John 17:17). Therefore, we all must labor to get into the Word of God.

First Timothy 5:17 says that the elders must do two things: take the lead well and labor in the Word of God. Those who labor in the Word of God will be counted worthy of double honor.

Let me ask all of you, is it difficult to study? Last night I saw from my window some children who were studying until eleven o'clock. I want to ask you who love the Lord, do you labor in the Word of the Lord and study it as carefully as those children were studying? Is your lack of study because the church does not put you under pressure or give you examinations? Is it because the church does not give you a grade and a degree? As in the past, we may still think that it is sufficient if we merely come to the meetings, be a little zealous, and, once we become full-time, do nothing else but pick up our Bible bag every day, with no examinations and no passing or failing. We may still think that the co-workers have a lifelong tenure. Such a condition is abominable to the Lord.

TRUTH EDUCATION REQUIRING TEXTBOOKS AND A LARGE MEETING HALL

Therefore, I charge you: in order for the Lord's work, the Lord's recovery, the Lord's church, to have a way, there must be a group of people who labor in the Word of the Lord. The industries in Taiwan are so prosperous because thirty years ago the young people, who were then in their twenties, labored diligently in their studies. Today they have many accomplishments in science and industry. It is for this reason that the country has a future. These people who work in Taiwan are now in their forties and fifties. They have received the higher education provided by the government, and thus they have become useful and talented people. This is a very clear example. Today in the church our effort is not sufficient. We have been here in Taiwan for thirty-six years, but the results of our work cannot be compared to the results achieved in the industries of Taiwan. I gave a training here in 1952, and within a year over one hundred full-timers were raised up.

After I left Taiwan in 1960, there was no training, and not many full-timers were produced.

Praise the Lord that now you young people are rising up. I am concerned that you need teaching materials and textbooks. After you have the textbooks, you still need to work hard. Now I am concerned about two matters. The first matter is that we do not have any textbooks. After coming back to Taiwan this time, I have a strong burden to write textbooks. After the textbooks are written, you can all attend classes. My second concern is that we need to build a large meeting hall.

We must change the system. We cannot put together on the Lord's Day those who were saved thirty years ago and those who are saved today and give them the same message. If we were to preach week after week and year after year for thirty years, the Lord would still have no way. But if we change the system, if there are six hundred people coming to the meeting, we will need six rooms that can each hold one hundred people. We will need to divide the people into classes and give them different teaching materials. We cannot follow the denominations to build a meeting place, hire a resident pastor, then hire two more preachers and some janitors, train some members to sing in the choir, and have the Sunday service. If the Lord has mercy on us, in two or three years the large meeting hall can be built; then we can do many things. We must work hard to build up our spiritual education.

In the eight years of the Sino-Japanese War all the universities moved to inland China. There were no campus buildings; all the cottages and shacks became campus buildings. The notebooks were even made from toilet paper. Although the situation was like this, the university education was established. That is why China is so advanced today. In the same way, even though we are not well equipped today, having too little space and not enough manpower, we still must do our best. I hope that you brothers and sisters understand the real situation. What the Lord's church and the Lord's recovery need today is a group of people who know the truth. Not only a few co-workers and elders, but the majority of the brothers and sisters, must know the truth.

KNOWING THE ESSENCE OF GOD'S WORD

Now let us see the essence of God's Word in a simple way. If we want to know God's Word, we must know the essence of God's Word. The Word of God is the Bible. Its essence is:

The Divine Breath

God's Word is God's breathing out (2 Tim. 3:16). The Bible is God's breathing out; that is, it is the breath breathed out by God. The Bible is God's breathing. To God it is a matter of breathing out; to us it is a matter of breathing in. Through God's breathing out and our breathing in, God's word enters into us and becomes our life and life supply. Therefore, when we read the Bible, we must understand that the Bible is not merely black words on white paper, but it is the breathing out of God. It is full of spiritual breath. Therefore, we must not only understand the Bible with our mind, but we also must contact the word of the Bible with our spirit. Whenever we read the Bible we come to contact God.

The Spiritual Milk

The Bible is the spiritual milk. In 1 Peter 2:2 Peter said that we need to be like newborn babes desiring the guileless milk of the Word. In the Word of God there is the element of milk. This is also implied in Hebrews 5:12, which says, "You...have become those who have need of milk and not of solid food." God's Word is our spiritual breath; therefore, we must breathe it in. God's Word is also our milk; hence, we must drink it. We must desire the guileless milk of the Word.

The Bread of Life

God's Word is our bread of life, our food of life. This is indicated in Matthew 4:4, a word out of the Lord's mouth and a quote of Deuteronomy 8:3: "Man shall not live on bread alone, but on every word that proceeds out through the mouth of God." Therefore, whenever we read the Bible, we must breathe in the spiritual air, that is, the Spirit of God. We also must drink the spiritual milk and eat the bread of life, which is the Lord Himself

Spirit and Life

The Word of the Lord is spirit and life. In John 6:63 the Lord Jesus said, "The words which I have spoken unto you are spirit and are life."

Christ—God Himself

The Word is God. The consummation of the Word is Christ Himself, because Christ is the Word of God. John 1:1 says, "In the beginning was the Word...and the Word was God." This Word became flesh, and His name is Jesus Christ. Ultimately, the word in the Bible is God Himself. It is the embodiment of God Himself. This does not mean that we consider the words in black and white as the living God. What we mean is that the words in black and white contain God Himself. This God is Christ; He is our bread of life. This Christ is also the Spirit, who becomes our spiritual milk and our spiritual breath.

Therefore, when we come to read the Bible and learn to understand the Bible, we must have the attitude that the Bible is different from the textbooks in the schools. They are merely black words on white paper, simply a matter of knowledge. The essence of God's Word, however, is the breathing out of God, God's spiritual breath. God's Word is also the spiritual milk and the bread of life. It is spirit and life, and it is even God Himself. Therefore, we need to understand God's Word and also enter into the essence of God's Word.

We human beings are created; we have a body, a soul with thoughts, emotions, desires, and intentions, and a spirit. God cannot simply be the Spirit and enter into our spirit; this is too intangible and impossible for us to understand. Therefore, God has worked in a wonderful way. He has given us both the Bible and the Holy Spirit.

The Holy Spirit is contained within the Bible, and the Bible is carried within the Holy Spirit. They are mutually in one another; hence, the two are inseparable.

When we read the Bible, we touch the Spirit. When we touch the Spirit, the Bible is there as our practical support. We not only breathe in the spiritual breath, drink the spiritual drink, eat the spiritual food, and receive the Spirit and life, but we also have the clear Word to be our support, to satisfy our thinking and our thoughts. Here we can see the wonderful work of God. Not only do we have the Holy Spirit, but we also have the Bible. We cannot separate the two. If we read the Lord's Word daily, the Lord's Word will enter into us. Then we will know it and understand it.

CHAPTER TWO

THE WAY TO UNDERSTAND
THE WORD OF GOD

(1)

Scripture Reading: Eph. 6:17-18; Jer. 15:16; 1 Pet. 2:2;
2 Tim. 3:16; 2 Cor. 3:6

OUTLINE

II. The way to understand the Word of God:
   A. Understanding the Word of God literally.
   B. Pray-reading the Word of God with our spirit—
      Eph. 6:17-18.
   C. Eating, drinking, and breathing the Spirit and
      the life in the Word of God—Jer. 15:16; 1 Pet. 2:2;
      2 Tim. 3:16.
   D. Going beyond the letter, historical events, and
      persons and things to explore and to receive the
      revelation of life—2 Cor. 3:6.

The previous message was concerned with the essence
of God's Word. If we want to understand something, we
must know its essence. God's Word is God's breathing out.
It is also the spiritual milk and the food of life. It is spirit
and life. Ultimately, the Word is Christ, and it is also God
Himself. God's Word is not the sacred writing of a religion;
it is not philosophy, ethics, or theory. It is God's breathing
out of Himself; it is the spiritual milk and food; it is spirit
and life. It is just Christ—God Himself.

A MYSTERIOUS BOOK

Now we shall see the way to understand God's Word.
How can we understand God's Word? This is an important
question. The Bible is too mysterious. You may say that it
is simple. Indeed, it is quite simple. For this reason, some
say that the Bible cannot be regarded as the sacred writing

of a religion. They say that it only talks about common things. They do not know how mysterious and profound the Bible is. Hu Shih, the modern Chinese philosopher who during the May Fourth Movement strongly promoted the change of Chinese classical literature into the spoken style of writing, once said that the Chinese Bible is a great reformation in Chinese writing. This proves that he studied the Chinese Bible. However, he did not know anything concerning the truth and the gospel in the Bible, because he did not believe in the Lord. This proves that high education and knowledge cannot help a person to understand the Bible.

For example, a chicken is covered with feathers. Under the feathers is the chicken skin, and under the skin are the meat and bones. Furthermore, there may still be dung in the intestines of the chicken. However, when we eat the chicken, we eat only the chicken meat. According to my study of the Bible, I can say that there are "feathers," "skin," "bones," and "dung" in the Bible. Do not think that I am wrong. In the first chapter of Romans there are over twenty kinds of sins. In addition, the second chapter of Ephesians mentions not only the fallen sinners on earth, but also the ruler of the authority of the air, that is, the operating evil spirit, which is the power of darkness. Do you not think that these are "chicken dung?" Furthermore, the Bible not only has God's word but also the word of the old serpent, Satan. In chapter three of Genesis the serpent spoke to the woman.

The Bible is too mysterious. It is not like the books written by ordinary men. In it there are good things, bad things, heavenly things, earthly things, and even things under the earth. God is there, and the Devil is also there. Holy men are there, and so are sinners. The Bible includes everything. When we read it, it seems very simple. For example, in John 8:12 Jesus said, "I am the light of the world," and in John 6:35 He said, "I am the bread of life...and he who believes in Me shall by no means ever thirst." These are simple words, but within them are depths that men cannot comprehend. Therefore, it is not easy to study the Bible. For this reason, I would like to spend two messages on how to know the truths in the Bible. These messages are based not only on my studies but also on my personal experiences.

THE WAY TO UNDERSTAND THE WORD OF GOD

Understanding the Word of God Literally

When we read the Bible, the first way to understand the Word of God is to comprehend it literally. We must comprehend whatever the Bible says and never be distracted from the main thought. When we read the Bible, we should not interpret arbitrarily a passage that we do not understand, thus departing from the meaning of the Word. Many people study the Bible and spiritualize their interpretation of it. For example, John 3:5 says, "Unless a man is born of water and the Spirit..." There is a group of people who feel that "water" here is difficult to interpret, so they take it as a sign, a symbol, and assume that the water refers to God's word. According to Ephesians 5:26, which refers to "the water in the word," they say that to be born again one must first hear the word of God. When God's word comes to us, the Spirit also comes. Therefore, they say that to be born of water and the Spirit is to be born of the Spirit through the word. Although this kind of spiritualizing in the interpretation of the Bible is not bad and seems to be consistent with the Bible, it does have its problems. If this interpretation of John 3:5 were true, why did the Lord Jesus not tell Nicodemus plainly at the beginning that a man must be born of the word, instead of telling him that a man must be born of water? By asking such a question, we can see that the interpretation of "water" as "the word" is unacceptable. Thus, we can see that we need to try our best to understand the Bible literally.

To understand the Word of God literally, however, is not simple, and it also has its problems. For example, there is a group of people in the United States who interpret the new birth in John chapter three to mean that a person must be born twice, the first time from his mother's womb and the second time of the Spirit. This is the reason that the Lord Jesus spoke of these two things, the water and the Spirit. According to their interpretation, the water refers to the fluid that bathes the fetus in the mother's womb. A man, therefore, must be born first of the fluid in his mother's womb and then of the Spirit. Through these two births, he is born again. This kind of "literal interpretation" is very poor.

First of all, we must know to whom the Lord was speaking in John 3. He was speaking to Nicodemus. John 3:1 clearly indicates that Nicodemus was a Pharisee. When John the Baptist came to preach and to baptize people in water, he told the Pharisees, "I indeed baptize you in water unto repentance; but He Who is coming after me...shall baptize you in the Holy Spirit" (Matt. 3:11). In his speaking John already had put the water and the Spirit together. Therefore, Nicodemus must have understood the word of the Lord Jesus. Because of this, the Lord Jesus spoke to him in a straightforward way. This is to not interpret the Word literally in a natural way but to interpret it according to its right meaning in the context.

As John the Baptist put all the repentant persons into the water, their old man was buried and terminated. The Lord Jesus then followed this to enliven them with the Spirit. The water is for burial, and the Spirit is for resurrection. When the two are put together, we have death and resurrection. This is the meaning of being born again. I have used this example to show you the right way to interpret the Bible. In the next message I will tell you the two criteria for this kind of interpretation of the Bible. The first is to interpret the Bible with the word of the Bible, and the second is to interpret it according to the context. Those who interpret the water in John 3:5 as the fluid from the mother's womb do so because they have not studied the Bible thoroughly and have not paid attention to the context. They merely interpret the Word according to their natural understanding, and consequently they make a serious mistake.

I am using this opportunity to give you these basic rules, especially for the sake of the young brothers and sisters who still have a long future on this earth. You need to labor on the Word of the Lord. This Bible has been in the hands of Christians for nearly two thousand years. Tens of thousands of scholars have studied this book, but most of them have interpreted it in their own way. If we want to know the Bible, the first thing we must do is to comprehend it literally; then we must pay attention to the context.

Pray-reading the Word of God with Our Spirit

Second, we need to use our spirit to pray-read the Word of God. To comprehend the Word literally we first need to read the black and white letters with our eyes as well as with our mind. Second, we need to pray-read, converting all that we see and all that we comprehend into prayer. When we pray, we use our spirit. At first, we may use our mind to pray, but after three to five sentences our spirit will rise up. This is a definite fact. Therefore, never forget that the essence of the Word of God is God's breathing out. When you read it, you should breathe it in. On God's side, it is a matter of His breathing out; on our side, it is a matter of our breathing in. The spiritual breath comes out of Him and enters into us. That which comes out of Him and enters into us is the spiritual breath. The Word of God is spirit and life. Our mind cannot touch the Spirit; only our spirit can touch the Spirit. If we do not touch the Spirit, we do not have life. Only by touching the Spirit can we have life. Ultimately, this life is Christ, and it is also God Himself.

In the previous message we pointed out the essence of God's Word. This message teaches us how to practice to touch this essence. At first, we do not need to explain what we read, nor do we need to understand it; we only need to pray-read the Word literally. When we pray-read, our spirit touches the Spirit of the Bible, and thus we receive life. Many of you can testify to this. For example, a newly saved person may read the first chapter of the Gospel of Matthew. He may not read the footnotes, and he may not read the Life-studies. He may simply begin to pray-read from verse one: "Oh, Abraham; Oh, the son of Abraham. O

Lord, You are the son of Abraham, the son of David. Jesus Christ—Oh, Jesus; Oh, Christ; Jesus Christ. Abraham begot Isaac. Praise the Lord! Isaac begot Jacob..." If he prays like this for five or six minutes, his whole inner being will be very bright and clear, even though he may not understand anything. This is neither imagination nor superstition. We can prove this with the fact of our experience. The Bible is the Bible. Even if you pray-read Genesis 3:1-2, "Now the serpent was more subtile than any beast of the field which the Lord God had made. And he said unto the woman, Yea, hath God said...," your spirit will be nourished. This is truly marvelous.

Eating, Drinking, and Breathing the Spirit and the Life in the Word of God

The matter of pray-reading to eat, drink, and breathe the Spirit and the life in the Word of God is seen in the word of the Bible; hence, pray-reading is not superstitious. When we pray-read, the word in letters becomes spirit and life, that is, the Lord Himself. To pray-read is to receive "the sword of the Spirit, which is the word of God, by means of all prayer and petition" (Eph. 6:17-18). Whenever we receive the Word of God by pray-reading, the result is that we eat, drink, and breathe in the Spirit and the life in God's Word. Even an Old Testament saint, Jeremiah, also said, "Thy words were found, and I did eat them" (Jer. 15:16). The Word of God is edible; hence, it is our food. Therefore, we must "long for the guileless milk of the word" (1 Pet. 2:2). In Hebrews 5:12 we are told that the Word of God is of two kinds: milk for those who are babes, and solid food for those who are mature. In addition, God's Word is also God's breathing out. When we breathe in God's Word, breathing in what God has breathed out, we receive Him. It is clear, then, that to pray-read is to eat, to drink, and to breathe, and the more consistently we practice it, the better. If we eat a little, drink a little, and breathe a little, as time goes on we will be purified. Furthermore, we will go beyond the letter, the historical events, and the people and things, and we will obtain the revelation of life.

The Bible does have some "skins" and some "feathers," but within these things is the revelation of life. However, when we read the Bible, we are often hindered by the outward things. This is especially true when we read the Old Testament. For example, a man may read Genesis 1:1, "In the beginning God created the heaven and the earth." He may then read concerning God's creation of Adam and Eve. Up to this point his understanding may be quite good. However, when he reads about Abraham, he may not be able to understand, and he may think, "Abraham is a holy man seeking after God. How could he treat his wife in this way? His wife is Sarah; then how could he take Hagar as his concubine? Having done this, how can he be the father of the saints?" Therefore, he has problems in studying the Bible. Later on he may read about the Israelites coming out of Egypt, entering into Canaan, and destroying the seven tribes in Canaan. Then he may think, "God is not fair. How could He have helped the Israelites to kill the seven tribes in Canaan?" I have heard all these questions, and I have also had to answer them.

This also applies to the reading of the New Testament. People either read it wrongly or become obsessed with certain matters in their reading. For example, John 13 mentions that we should wash one another's feet. There are people who insist on the practice of foot washing and cannot do without it. Because of this, they have a foot washing group and wash one another's feet every Sunday. This is going too far. First Corinthians 11 speaks of the need for women to cover their heads. Some people consider this to be merely an ancient custom, and they maintain that it should not be regarded as a commandment to be taught to others. Furthermore, some people speak against what they consider to be the unfair treatment of women in 1 Corinthians 14:34-35, which says, "Let the women be silent in the churches, for they are not permitted to speak." Again, they consider this as an old religious practice that is now out-of-date. Indeed, the study of the Bible does present these kinds of difficulties. Not only so, but there are people who even find fault with the Lord Jesus. For example, at one time Jesus said to His mother, "Woman, what have I to do with you?" (John 2:4). Many Chinese readers would feel that, since their country was founded upon human morality and ethics, they would never teach their children to speak to their mothers as the Lord Jesus did. Furthermore, on another occasion, when someone told Jesus that His mother and His brothers had come to seek Him, He answered by saying, "Who is My mother, and who are My brothers?... for whoever does the will of My Father Who is in the heavens, he is My brother and sister and mother" (Matt. 12:48-50). When they read this passage, some people think that Jesus was insane. From these cases we can see that many people's way of studying the Bible indeed has these difficulties.

Going Beyond the Letter, Historical Events, and Persons and Things to Explore and to Receive the Revelation of Life

In order to study the Bible, we must go beyond the letter, that is, the letter in the law. For example, the Seventh Day Adventists hold on to the letter in the Bible: "Remember the sabbath day, to keep it holy." However, Paul said, "The letter kills, but the Spirit gives life" (2 Cor. 3:6). This word should be applied to the matter of the keeping of the Sabbath. "The letter" requires people to keep the Sabbath, but the spiritual meaning of keeping the Sabbath is that God wants whoever is laboring and is burdened to obtain rest. Hence, it is not a matter of keeping the letter, but of receiving the Spirit. According to the spiritual meaning, the Sabbath is the rest that God has established for those who are heavily burdened, and this Sabbath is just the Lord Christ. It is not surprising that the Lord said, "Come to Me all who labor and are burdened, and I will give you rest" (Matt. 11:28). This is today's Sabbath. Similarly, regarding the matter of circumcision, to require people to be circumcised on the eighth day is merely the letter. The spiritual meaning of circumcision is to terminate our flesh, to deny our natural life. The letter kills, but the Spirit gives life. The Spirit goes beyond the letter and also beyond the historical events. Although Sarah, the wife of Abraham, and Hagar, Abraham's concubine, did not have positive histories, Paul went beyond the historical facts to see the revelation contained within them. He spoke of these two women as two covenants. Galatians chapter four reveals that Sarah, the wife of Abraham, represents the covenant of grace, whereas Hagar symbolizes the covenant of law. From this we can see that in the Bible the position of the law is like that of a concubine, whereas the position of grace is like that of the real wife.

Let us return to the incident recorded in John 2:4, in which the Lord Jesus called His own mother "Woman." When we go beyond the historical events, we can see the spiritual revelation of life. The Lord Jesus was God incarnated to become flesh; He was the Son of God. Outwardly, He was born of Mary according to the flesh; hence, He was the Son of Man. However, He was in fact the Son of God inwardly.

The Bible is mysterious. We all must go beyond the historical events and persons in order to see the revelation of life hidden within them.

CHAPTER THREE

THE WAY TO UNDERSTAND THE WORD OF GOD

(2)

OUTLINE

III. The way to understand the Word of God:
  E. Taking care of the context.
  F. Expounding God's Word with God's Word.
  G. Learning from the saints of the past:
    1. Relying on the teaching that the Brethren have received (the higher theology).
    2. Knowing thoroughly the inner life teaching.
    3. Receiving Calvin's revelation concerning predestination.
    4. Refusing the insistence of Arminianism on human responsibility.
    5. Holding the balance of the truth concerning the kingdom reward and punishment.

GOD'S DISPENSING BEING THE CENTER OF THE REVELATION OF THE BIBLE

In this message we shall learn how to read the Word of God practically. We all know that the Bible is the Word of God and that it is extremely mysterious and all-inclusive. Its most central point is to reveal God Himself to us. The purpose of this revelation is not merely that we may know God, as is often emphasized by Christians, but much more that He may work Himself into us. The way He accomplishes this is through dispensing. Even though we cannot find the word "dispensing" in the Bible, still the fact of dispensing is in the Bible, just as the term "the Triune God" is not in the Bible, yet there is the fact of the Triune God.

How can we prove this? Second Corinthians 13:14 says,

"The grace of the Lord Jesus Christ, and the love of God, and the fellowship of the Holy Spirit be with you all." Here we can see that when love comes, this love becomes grace, and when grace comes to us, it comes through fellowship; this is dispensing. Moreover, in Romans 8 we can even see the steps of this dispensing. First, Christ, the life-giving Spirit, who is God Himself, comes into our spirit, causing our spirit to have the life of God (v. 10). Then He desires to enter into our mind, which is the major part of our soul, so that our soul may have the life of God (v. 6). Last, He supplies His life to our body (v. 11). Thus our spirit, soul, and body all have His life. This process is God's dispensing. This is the central and major point in the Bible. The divine Trinity is for the dispensing of God Himself into us.

GOD PASSING THROUGH FIVE STEPS

God desires to dispense Himself into us. However, this is not so simple that it can be accomplished in one step. In order to do this, God had to pass through steps and processes beyond human imagination. He had to take at least five steps, and He had to complete some great accomplishments. The first step was incarnation. God became flesh, which was not a simple matter. The Creator of the universe, almighty God, has now become flesh! We must realize that in the Bible, the word "flesh" does not mean the untouched, undamaged man; rather, it refers to the fallen, defiled, and damaged man. This Triune God, the Creator of the universe, came in the likeness of such a man—in the likeness of the flesh of sin (Rom. 8:3)—through incarnation. No wonder the Bible says that He had "no form nor comeliness" (Isa. 53:2).

The second step of God's process was His passing through human living. I often say that it took Him at most nine months to become incarnated, but His human living lasted for thirty-three and a half years. In particular, the first thirty years of His life were not a small thing. It was not a simple matter for the unlimited God, the Lord of all, to be in such a lowly Person, Jesus, on the earth in a small town, Nazareth, in the home of a carpenter for thirty years.

Bible scholars seldom see this. I have listened to many ministries for many years, yet I have never heard anyone give a sermon on this subject.

The third step was His crucifixion. His death was not a common death, and it is difficult to explain. On the one hand, He was killed by man, as Peter testified, "And the Author of life you killed" (Acts 3:15a). But on the other hand, the Lord Himself said concerning His life, "No one takes it away from Me, but I lay it down of Myself" (John 10:18a). Who could ever capture Him unless He was willing to die? In the garden of Gethsemane, the officials of the temple in Jerusalem came with soldiers to find Jesus, the Nazarene. When Jesus said, "I am," they all drew back and fell to the ground (John 18:6). When Peter drew a sword and cut off the ear of the slave of the high priest, the Lord said, "Put the sword into the sheath" (John 18:11). This indicates that He was willing to give Himself up to man.

On the cross, He died a sevenfold death and terminated all the negative things in the universe, including sin, Satan, the world, the old creation, the old man, the flesh, and the ordinances of the law, which were against us. This is on the negative side. On the positive side, His all-inclusive death released the divine life that was in Him. This is like a flower seed which falls into the ground. Once it receives moisture, its outer shell begins to rot; this is a kind of death. When such a death occurs, the inner life of the seed begins to germinate. The more the shell dies, the more the inner life germinates. When the shell dies completely, the inner life's germination will also be completed; thus a tender sprout will grow out. This shows that death releases life. Our Lord Jesus was such a seed sown into the ground. As His outward body was dying, His inner life was germinating (1 Pet. 3:18), allowing Him to come out of Hades and the tomb. This was His resurrection. In resurrection He took another form; that is, He became the Spirit of life. This Spirit of life is still He, but in a different form, just as the flower seed and the sprout are really one thing, but in two different stages.

The fourth step of His process was resurrection. When Christ entered into resurrection, He brought us also into resurrection (Eph. 2:5-6). At the same time, He also became the life-giving Spirit (1 Cor. 15:45b). Having passed through the four steps of incarnation, human living, crucifixion, and resurrection, He ascended to the heavens. It was not only the Lord of all, but the Man of Nazareth, who went to the throne in the heavens. How wonderful! Incarnation is God entering into man, and resurrection is man entering into God. While He was living the human life, it was God who was on the earth; when He ascended to the heavens, it was a Man who entered into the heavens. Hallelujah! God was on the earth for thirty-three and a half years; today a Man is in the heavens. Then it was God who was living on the earth; today it is a Man who is living in the heavens.

OUR NEED OF ENLIGHTENMENT
TO KNOW THE BIBLE

This is the process of five steps that our God, the Triune God, passed through. By His coming and going, He brought God into man and man into God. God lived a life on the earth, and a Man now lives a life in the heavens. This is the revelation of the Bible. The Lord Jesus, in whom we believe, is such a Lord. In these last days it is His mercy to make all these details clear to us. When I preached these things in the United States, the leading Christian country, many theologians and Bible scholars were pierced in their hearts. They falsely accused me, saying that since I am an old Chinaman, I preach oriental thought and old Chinese philosophies. Some even said that I am a pantheist, that I consider everything as God. What darkness they are in! To this day no prominent theologian or professor of theology has written a proper book to refute my theological viewpoints. Today, the whole of Christianity is in darkness. In other words, they know almost nothing of the truth. We need to know that obtaining a doctor's degree in Hebrew and Greek does not mean that one knows the Bible. Many of these people are even unbelievers; they read the Bible with blind eyes. It is not sufficient to know the Bible in the way of understanding the meaning of each word in the original language; we must see the light revealed by the meaning of each word in the original language.

For example, when the Sadducees argued with the Lord Jesus, saying that there was no resurrection, the Lord Jesus answered, "Concerning the dead, that they are raised, did you not read in the book of Moses, at the bush, how God spoke to him, saying, I am the God of Abraham, and the God of Isaac, and the God of Jacob?" (Mark 12:26). In reading the phrase "the God of Abraham, and the God of Isaac, and the God of Jacob," the Lord saw the matter of resurrection. He said, "He is not the God of the dead, but of the living" (v. 27). Apparently these men are dead, but since God is the God of Abraham, the God of Isaac, and the God of Jacob, they will be resurrected. This was the way in which the Lord Jesus read the Bible. He had the divine light. To study the Bible, we need light, which does not come by studying the letters. If we desire to go beyond the letters and seek the revelation of life, we need enlightenment.

Today's theology is very shallow and superficial. It seems that theologians only skate on the ice and are not willing to break the ice and dive into the ocean to explore the depths. Even the hymns used by today's Christianity are shallow and superficial. We are sorry to say that today's Christianity is so shallow and knows so little. Today we are here to be trained. I surely have a burden, especially for you young people. I really treasure the fact that you have dropped everything in order to learn to serve the Lord and to study His Word. Today I am here to have an honest talk with my family. I have to say that the blindness and shallowness of today's Christianity have wasted many people's time and even their whole lives. I was born in Christianity and have been involved with many aspects of Christianity, such as organized Christianity, fundamental Christianity, the inner life movement, the Brethren, and the Pentecostals. I cannot say that I have read all the books of Christianity; however, with sixty years of experience, I know most of the different denominations well. I have experienced and seen many things. I was born in China and worked for the Lord in Shanghai, the largest city in China. I have been in Taiwan, Southeast Asia, and America. I have been to all of the six continents except Africa. I hold no degrees, and I do not know Hebrew. I know only enough Greek to be able to use reference books. But I cannot deny one fact: that today's Christianity is desolate, shallow, and ignorant of the truth. You can discern this by looking at their hymns. Even their best writings are very shallow.

GAINING LIFE THROUGH PRAY-READING

Concerning the matter of understanding God's Word, I have mentioned four points. First, we must understand God's Word literally. Second, whereas literal comprehension requires that we use our eyes and our mind, we also need to use our spirit to pray-read God's Word. The Word of God is the bread of life and the spiritual milk; it is also God's breathing out. Since it is food, we need to eat it; since it is milk, we need to drink it; and since it is breath, we need to breathe it in. By pray-reading we are able to eat, drink, and breathe. This is what is lacking among many Christians today. They exhaust their minds to study the letter of the Bible, but they do not use their spirit to pray-read the Word of God. Therefore, Jesus said to the Pharisees, "You search the Scriptures...and you are not willing to come to Me that you may have life" (John 5:39-40). To study the Scriptures is one thing, but to come to the Lord by prayer to touch Him and gain His life is totally another matter. The common problem of today's theological seminaries is that they place too much emphasis on mental exercise to study the letter of the Bible in a doctrinal way, thus neglecting the use of their spirit to pray-read the Word.

I read a book about a contemporary of John Wesley named George Whitefield. His preaching was even more powerful than that of Wesley. He prayed on his knees over the Greek New Testament from beginning to end. His biography mentions that whenever he preached the gospel or ministered God's Word, he prayed for a long time beforehand over what he would say. No wonder his preaching was so full of authority and power! One day he was speaking about hell. He described it so vividly that one person from the congregation stood up quickly and ran to a huge column in the assembly hall. He held onto the column and cried, "Oh! Be careful, or else we will all fall into the lake of fire!" Whitefield's preaching was so powerful that it seemed that he was presenting the lake of fire before the eyes of the congregation.

BEING CLEANSED BY PRAY-READING

The matter of pray-reading the Lord's Word is not a theory. We read the Word with our eyes and comprehend the letters with our mind; then we need to use our spirit to pray-read the Word. You may try this not only with Bible passages of comforting and enlightening words; even pray-reading the genealogy in the first chapter of Matthew a few times will cause you to sense the painting of the inner anointing, just as drinking a good beverage will make you feel fresh and living. On one occasion, someone said to Brother Nee, "I do not have a good memory, and I often forget the verses which I just read. It seems that I am wasting my time. What I read in the morning I will forget by the evening; I might just as well not read the Bible at all." Brother Nee answered, "No, it makes a great difference whether or not you read. You see, it is just as one cleans rice in a bamboo basket in a pond. When the basket is immersed, it is full of water. But when it is taken out of the pond, the water is gone. By repeating the process of immersing the basket and taking it out of the water eight or ten times, the rice is washed. When you get up in the morning, you read the Bible and pray a little; but later, after working for two hours, you have forgotten all the verses which you have read. Yes, the words are gone, but the effectiveness of the washing still remains."

Therefore, in reading the Bible we do not need to understand it too clearly in our mind. Exercising our mind too much might distort the meaning of the Bible. The most important thing is to let our spirit be fed. Every morning we should immerse ourselves in the water of the Lord's Word eight or ten times. Two hours later we may become dry again. But even though there is no more water, neither is there any more dirt; we have been cleansed. Therefore, when we read the Lord's Word, having used our mind to understand it, immediately we should turn to prayer. Do not think that you are smart and can compose a prayer by yourself. Let me tell you, young people, the best way to pray is to use the words of the Bible. For example, we can convert Matthew 1:1 into a prayer: "O Lord Jesus! I worship You. I love You, Son of Abraham. O Lord Jesus, You are the Son of Abraham. How precious! You are also the Son of David. Oh, the Son of David! Lord Jesus, Son of David! The generation of Jesus Christ. Jesus—the name is so sweet! Oh, Christ—the name is so high! Jesus Christ. Jesus Christ, amen. Jesus, amen. Christ, amen. Jesus Christ, amen!"

Brothers and sisters, the letter kills, but the Spirit gives life. We have to read the letter, because this is how the Bible is written, and we have to use our mind to comprehend. However, we must convert the letter of the Bible into prayer. Once they have been converted into prayer, God's words become spirit and life. Not only so, we also need to take a further step: having understood and prayed over the words, we need to seek the revelation of life by going beyond the letters.

THE WAY TO UNDERSTAND GOD'S WORD

Paying Attention to the Context in Reading the Bible

Now we will continue what we talked about in the previous message concerning the matter of taking care of the context in our reading of the Bible. It is very dangerous to neglect the context. For example, Psalm 14:1 says, "The fool hath said in his heart, There is no God. They are corrupt...." If we omit the first and the last parts of this verse, all that is left is, "There is no God." Many people expound and understand the Bible in such a way. Those friends who accuse me of preaching heresy usually slander me by this method. They take sentences out of context in order to misinterpret my writings.

Paying attention to the context requires much consideration, because there are no specific limits as to the boundary of a passage. A prominent Bible scholar has said that in order to expound a single sentence of the Bible, one needs to use the entire Bible. This means that we need all sixty-six books of the Bible to explain a verse. For example, in Matthew 18:20 the Lord said, "For where two or three are gathered together into My name, there I am in their midst." I would say that this verse concerns the building up of the local church. How can I be so bold to say this? Because the entire context of Matthew 18 reveals this. Not only so, if we read the entire context of this chapter, we must admit that the Lord's word "gathered together into My name" is related to recovering the brothers who have committed wrongdoings, and this is surely for building up. In chapter sixteen, the Lord said, "On this rock I will build My church" (v. 18), but He did not mention there how to build the church. Chapter eighteen, however, reveals to us that the way to build the church is to gather together into the name of the Lord. Not a great number of saints, but a small number, even two or three, may meet together to recover some brothers. To recover the brothers is to build up the brothers. To make peace, to forgive, and to be understanding of the brothers is the building up. If three thousand or even five hundred people meet together with one person preaching and others listening, after the dismissal of the meeting no one knows whether there are any complaints, discontent, or other problems. There is no building. However, when three or five saints are gathered together, everything is out in the open, and nothing can be hidden; therefore, there is a need for fellowship, restoration, peacemaking, and understanding. This is the true building up. We can have such a definitive interpretation of these verses in Matthew 18 because of their context. Therefore, I would say that studying the Bible is not a simple matter, and comprehending the Bible is even more difficult. In order to comprehend one verse, you may have to research the entire Bible. It is just like a lawyer who cannot make a decision on a legal case according to only a single code of the law. In fact, all the codes are related to each other. A good lawyer is one who not only knows the law in depth but also can assimilate and use it in a comprehensive manner.

Using God's Word to Expound God's Word

In general, Bible scholars use the Word of God to explain God's Word; this is to use the Bible to interpret the Bible. For example, some may interpret the word "water" in John 3:5 in a spiritual way, considering the water as God's word, because according to James 1:18, God "brought us forth by the word of truth." First Peter 1:23 says, "Having been regenerated, not of corruptible seed, but of incorruptible, through the living and abiding word of God." Ephesians also mentions "the water in the word" (5:26). We have already pointed out that this exposition of the word "water" in John 3:5 is not right; it is not according to the literal meaning of the word but is interpreted in a spiritual way. Others even say that this "water" is the water in a mother's womb. This interpretation is too literal. It is not wrong to expound the Word literally, but it must be done not in a natural way or according to human concepts. From the context of this verse, we can see that the Lord Jesus was speaking to Nicodemus, a Pharisee, who must have heard what John the Baptist had said to the Pharisees: "I indeed baptize you with water, but He who is stronger than I is coming.... He will baptize you in the Holy Spirit" (Luke 3:16). Thus, we must have a way to determine the appropriate context of a verse. When the Lord Jesus said to Nicodemus that he must be "born of water and the Spirit," He meant, "You must accept the baptism of repentance preached by John the Baptist. First you must repent; then he will put you fully into the water to bury you, and I will come after him to baptize you with the Spirit to enliven you." This is death and resurrection. The old man dies and is buried, and the new man is resurrected. Is this not the real significance of being born anew? So you see, this interpretation is according to the literal understanding, yet not in the natural way. Therefore, whenever you encounter a sentence in the Bible and you do not understand its meaning, do not try to figure it out by thinking this way or that way. You should go to the entire Bible to see what is said concerning this sentence; that is to use the words of the Bible to expound the Word.

Learning from the Saints of the Past

We also need to learn from the saints of the past. We must realize that we were not born in the first century; we are not the first group of Bible readers. We were born in the twentieth century, and we cannot ignore those who have gone before us. We cannot work in isolation from them. We must see how the so-called church fathers, from the end of the first century to the second century, interpreted the Bible. Since then, in generation after generation there have been Bible scholars. During the time of the Reformation, Wycliffe and his contemporaries rose up; then Luther consummated their teachings. They all had various interpretations concerning the Bible. Afterwards, a number of different schools emerged. Today we are standing on their shoulders, and a great deal of our knowledge of the Bible has been gained from them.

Some Important Schools of Theology

In the twentieth century, the schools of theology we have studied, either in the West or in the East, can be classified as follows: The first is secular theology. It is difficult to find this kind of theology in China. In the United States most of the large, well-known universities have divinity schools. These schools are not theological seminaries. They study theology as a kind of literature with a certain cultural background. This kind of secular theology is bad, but there is a still worse kind, which is called modern or liberal theology. Liberal theologians do not recognize the authority of the Bible or the existence of God as revealed in the Bible. They do not accept the fact that the Lord Jesus is God, nor do they believe in miracles, angels, or Satan. Their belief is very much like that of the Sadducees (Acts 23:8).

Besides these, there is also the orthodox theology represented by many theological seminaries. Every denomination has its own seminaries, and their teachings differ one from another. Nevertheless, although their emphases are different, their fundamental theological views are nearly the same. They all accept the authority of the Bible as the Word of God. They believe that God is unique, yet He is three in one; that the Lord Jesus is the Son of God incarnated to become man; and that He died on the cross for us, not for martyrdom but for our redemption. They believe that He resurrected bodily and spiritually, then ascended to the heavens and is now sitting on the throne, and that today He is the Savior, the King of kings and Lord of lords. All these are the basic beliefs of the theology of the so-called fundamentalists.

There is still another theology which has been regarded as one of the schools among the fundamentalists, that is, reformed theology. However, those who teach it hold a major doctrine which is erroneous to the point of being heretical: they do not believe that the believers have two natures. We know that before we were saved we inherited the old nature from Adam, and after regeneration we received a new life and a new nature from God. Therefore, we have two natures, the nature of the old man and the nature of the new man. This doctrine is totally scriptural. Yet reformed theology, instead of saying that we have two natures, says that our original nature is old but gradually will be improved into a new nature. There is a great danger hidden in this teaching: it implicitly denies the fact of regeneration. Reformed theology also says that the millennial kingdom is a condition which will be achieved on earth before the second coming of our Lord through gradual improvement. It says that although mankind is wicked and fallen at the present time, men can be gradually improved through the teachings of the Bible and the preaching of the gospel. This theology was prevailing prior to the First World War; but the sudden outbreak of

THE WAY TO UNDERSTAND THE WORD OF GOD   41

the war in Europe totally annulled their teaching. After the war, people dared not to talk too much about this doctrine. Then the Second World War came, and the fighting was more intense; thus they became even more uncertain as to how the Lord Jesus could come back. Even today reformed theologians still believe that teaching the truth and preaching the gospel can change human society and cause it to gradually advance into a utopia. This utopia is equal to the millennial kingdom. This doctrine is erroneous, heretical, and unacceptable.

The Highest Theology

In addition, during the first half of the last century, in the late 1820s, the Lord raised up the Brethren in England. They had many Bible teachers; the first among them was John Nelson Darby. There were also C. H. Mackintosh and William Kelly. First, they unlocked many biblical principles; second, they unlocked the types; third, they unlocked the prophecies; fourth, they unlocked the dispensations; and fifth, they unlocked the proper knowledge concerning the Triune God and the Person of Christ. Finally, they also unlocked the truth concerning the church. These are the six conclusions we can obtain through their writings.

First, they unlocked the principles of the Bible. There is one set of principles for the books of the Old Testament and another set of principles for the books of the New Testament. The culmination of Darby's writings was the five-volume commentary on the Bible called *Synopsis of the Books of the Bible*. He abstracted every book in the Bible and found the underlying principles in each book. This was his greatest strength; this was also where I received the most help.

Second, the Brethren dug out the types in the Bible. While reading the New Testament, they picked up all the related verses. For example, Romans 5:14 says that Adam is a type of Christ. Galatians 4 says that Abraham had a wife named Sarah and a concubine named Hagar. These two women signify two testaments, the new testament and the old testament. In the Gospels the Lord Jesus also said,

"Behold, a greater than Solomon is here" (Matt. 12:42), "Have you not read what David did" (Matt. 12:3), and "A greater than Jonah is here" (Matt. 12:41). Solomon, David, and Jonah in the Old Testament are types of the Lord Jesus. When we read the New Testament in this way we will spontaneously realize that there are many shadows, types, and prophecies in the Old Testament describing the things in the New Testament. Generally speaking, it was the Brethren teachers who unlocked the types in the Old Testament. This was the greatest help which I received from meeting with them for seven and a half years.

Third, they unlocked the prophecies. The prophecies in the Bible can be divided into two categories. The first category consists of the prophecies concerning the Lord Jesus; these are the prophecies with promises. For example, Genesis 3:15 says that the seed of the woman will bruise the serpent's head. This is a prophecy, but it is also a promise. Then, in Genesis 22, God said to Abraham, "And in thy seed shall all the nations of the earth be blessed" (v. 18). Here the word "seed" refers to one Person, Christ (Gal. 3:16). Later, this prophecy and promise were also used to refer to the seed of Isaac (Gen. 26:2-4), the seed of Jacob (Gen. 28:13-14), and the seed of Judah. Genesis 49 says that Judah is a lion who will reign and has gone up from the prey. This prefigures Christ. Then in 2 Samuel God promised that David would have a son who would reign as a king, and that His kingdom would last forever (7:12-13).

The book of Isaiah prophesies, "Behold, a virgin shall conceive, and bear a son, and shall call his name Immanuel" (7:14). "For unto us a child is born, unto us a son is given... his name shall be called... The mighty God, The everlasting Father..." (9:6). The entire fifty-third chapter of Isaiah is full of prophecies and promises. There is no place in the New Testament which gives as clear an account of the gospel of Christ as Isaiah 53. Then Jeremiah 33 prophesies that Christ as God's righteousness will become our righteousness (vv. 15-16). The book of Daniel prophesies that Messiah will be cut off (9:26a); this refers to the crucifixion of the Lord Jesus. Then Hosea 11:1

says, "I...called my son out of Egypt"; this also refers to Christ. Micah 5:2 says "Whose goings forth have been from of old, from everlasting." Then we find more prophecies in Zechariah: Christ is referred to as the wounded One (13:6), the One the Jews have pierced (12:10), and the smitten Shepherd (13:7). In Haggai He is referred to as the desire of all nations (2:7). Finally, Malachi 4:2 prophesies that He will rise as the Sun of righteousness. In addition, the book of Psalms also has many prophecies concerning Christ's incarnation, crucifixion, resurrection, ascension, and enthronement.

The second kind of prophecy in the Old Testament is concerning the world situation, the people of the world, the Jews, the Gentiles, and the church. Pember wrote four volumes on the interpretation of prophecies. The first volume deals with the prophecies concerning the world; the second, with the prophecies concerning the Jews; the third, with the prophecies concerning the Gentiles; and the fourth, with the prophecies concerning the church. These prophecies are recorded in Daniel and Revelation. Some can also be found in Matthew 24, Luke 21, and other books.

The Brethren told us that in order to interpret these prophecies, one must maintain two governing principles. First, in Daniel 2 there is a great image, the head of which is of fine gold; the arms, of silver; the belly, of brass; the legs, of iron; and the feet, partly of iron and partly of clay. It also has ten toes. This image represents the history of the world. Babylon is represented by the golden head, Medo-Persia by the arms, Alexander's Greece by the brass belly, and the Eastern and Western Roman Empires by the two iron legs. With the passing of the Roman Empire, the idea of democracy began to spread. The French Revolution represents the coming of clay, when kings could no longer practice totalitarianism. Gold, silver, brass, and iron are metals which signify emperors. Clay signifies the people, the common man. But clay contains iron, which is stronger than clay. This is today's situation, partly of iron and partly of clay. Although democracy has been promoted, the practices of dictatorship and totalitarianism still prevail.

This great image is the principle by which the Bible explains the world situation, and we cannot go beyond it.

The second principle is the matter of the seventy weeks in Daniel 9. One week represents seven years. Seventy weeks are four hundred ninety years. The first sixty-nine weeks, totalling four hundred eighty-three years, began from the day Artaxerxes the king commanded the rebuilding of Jerusalem and ended with the crucifixion of the Lord Jesus. According to history, the day of the Lord Jesus' crucifixion was exactly the last day of the four hundred eighty-three years. In summary, we must have the great image in Daniel 2 and the seventy weeks in Daniel 9 as two lines; then we can properly interpret the prophecies of the Bible.

Two Opposing Schools

In addition, there are also two theological schools. One is the Calvinist school of predestination, which I call the revelation of God's predestination. Calvin saw that our salvation was not initiated by ourselves, but rather that we have been selected and predestinated by God before the foundation of the world (Eph. 1:4-5). This predestination is eternal and unchangeable; therefore, the saved ones will never perish. On the other hand, those of the Arminian school believe that whether we are saved eternally or not depends upon ourselves, that is, that we are responsible for our salvation. Therefore, we must do our best to walk according to God's will, or else we may still perish. I call this "elevator salvation": when we are saved we are up; when we sin we are down. The Baptist church accepts Calvin's revelation of God's predestination, and so do the Presbyterians. The Pentecostals, holiness groups, and the Assemblies of God are mostly Arminian in that they emphasize human responsibility and ignore God's selection. This is heresy. Calvin saw the revelation of God's predestination, and this is right.

These two schools are always in conflict with each other. The Arminian doctrine is mainly based upon the five warnings recorded in Hebrews and the warnings given by the Lord Jesus in the Gospel of Matthew. For example, if we fail to be a faithful servant, when the Master comes back, we will be punished and cast into outer darkness, where there will be the weeping and the gnashing of teeth (Matt. 24:45-51; 25:14-30). Based upon these verses, they claim that even a saved one can perish.

Later, people like Govett, Panton, and Pember rose up. Their doctrine stands between the revelation of God's predestination and the teaching of human responsibility. They saw the truth concerning the kingdom. They said that after being saved, we are saved forever and will never perish. But we must follow the Lord faithfully; then when the Lord comes back, we will receive the kingdom as a reward. If we are not faithful, we will not be able to enter the kingdom and we will suffer loss. This is based on 1 Corinthians 3, which says that we should be careful about how we build (vv. 10-15). Are we building with gold, silver, and precious stones, or are we building with wood, grass, and stubble? If we build with gold, silver, and precious stones, when the Lord comes back, we will be rewarded in addition to our salvation. On the other hand, if we build with wood, grass, and stubble, our work will be burned by the fire of judgment, and we will suffer loss but not eternal perdition: "But he shall be saved, yet so as through fire" (1 Cor. 3:15). Many proofs in the New Testament concerning the kingdom reward and punishment were initially seen by Govett and Panton.

What I have mentioned thus far is not my imagination. I am also a student of the Bible. I have studied this book for sixty years; this is why I am able to explain it to you. The Bible expositors of the past can be grouped into these several schools. We have studied them and would like to present them to you for your learning. When we began to expound the Bible, we profited a great deal from the saints before us. We have seen that the highest theology is that held by the Brethren. Once you have their theology, you can put aside all the others. What I have said is based on this high theology. Brothers and sisters, all that I have spoken to you describes the way of studying the Bible which we have learned during the past sixty years.

CHAPTER FOUR

SOME IMPORTANT ITEMS OF THE TRUTH THAT HAVE BEEN MISUNDERSTOOD

(1)

Scripture Reading: 1 Tim. 1:4; Eph. 3:9-11; 1:9-10; 3:2-4;
Col. 1:25-27; Eph. 3:8; 2 Cor. 13:14; Eph. 3:10; 1:23; 3:19

OUTLINE

IV. Some important items of the truth that have been misunderstood:
   A. God's economy—1 Tim. 1:4:
      1. God's household administration, arrangement, and plan—Eph. 3:9-11.
      2. The stewardship of God's household administration:
         a. Understanding the mystery of Christ (the church)—Eph. 3:2-4.
         b. Completing the word of God, that is, the mystery which has been hidden from the ages and from the generations, the glory of which is Christ in the believers, the hope of glory—Col. 1:25-27.
         c. Preaching to people the unsearchable riches of Christ—Eph. 3:8.
   B. God's dispensing:
      1. The goal of God's economy.
      2. In the rich operation of the Triune God, to dispense the unsearchable riches of Christ to the believers—Eph. 3:8; 2 Cor. 13:14.
      3. For the producing of the church—Eph. 3:10.
      4. To become the fullness of Christ and the fullness of God, to be the expression of God—Eph. 1:23; 3:19.

LEARNING FROM THE EXAMPLES
OF THE EARLY SAINTS

Beginning from this morning we are in "graduate school" and the lessons are weighty. The first thing we need to mention is that today, in the twentieth century, if we want to know the Bible, we need to learn from the examples of the early saints. Many Bible scholars raised up by the Lord had a thorough understanding of the Bible. Their labor in studying the Bible may have greatly surpassed ours. By reading their books, we know that they labored much.

BEFORE AND AFTER THE COUNCIL OF NICAEA

Let us consider the church fathers before the Council of Nicaea. These were the Bible scholars prior to the time that the Roman Empire adopted Christianity as the state religion. In 324 A.D. Constantine gained sole possession of the Roman Empire. He was foresighted and very talented. At that time many of the peoples surrounding the Mediterranean Sea were under the rule of the Roman Empire. Because of the ease of transportation, Greek spontaneously became the popular language in the Mediterranean region, just as English is over much of the world today. The Roman highways along the Mediterranean Sea allowed traffic to flow smoothly between Europe and Asia. However, because the domain of the Roman Empire was so broad and because it had so many territories, most of the people remained isolated.

Among all the peoples of the Roman Empire, the most powerful group was the Christians. Yet even among them there was little oneness. The church fathers had much debate on the essential truths of the Bible, concentrating on two main subjects: the Triune God and the person of Christ. Because of their fierce debating, in 325 A.D. Constantine ordered all the Christian teachers to come to Nicaea for a council over which he presided. At that council many Bible scholars debated over previous writings. From that time until about 570 A.D., approximately 250 years, a number of councils were held, and some arguments concerning the truth were settled.

Today the Roman Catholic and Greek Orthodox churches believe not only the Bible but also various creeds. The creeds are the resolutions of all the councils. Of course, the creeds come from the Bible, but they are only a supplement to the Bible, at the most just something auxiliary. There is still quite a separation between the creeds and the Bible. It is very difficult to include all the sixty-six books in a creed. The creed which was the product of the Council of Nicaea only includes a part of the Bible; yet today many Protestants still recite the Nicene Creed in their worship. One group even has a slogan admonishing people to go back to the Council of Nicaea and to accept its resolution. Nevertheless, we cannot deny the fact that the church fathers did much in-depth study of the Bible prior to the Council of Nicaea. After the church fathers passed away, many Bible scholars who attended those councils also did much study.

THE DARK AGES

The medieval papacy was established in 590 A.D. Except for the Greek Orthodox church, all the churches became known as Roman churches. The highest bishop was the pope, meaning "old father," or "the presiding one." When the authority of the pope was fully established with the recognition of the churches, the Roman church became known as the Catholic church. At that time the Bible was locked up; the believers were not allowed to read the Bible. The pope was the sole arbiter. Under the pope were the cardinals, under the cardinals were the archbishops, and under the archbishops were the bishops, with all deferring to the pope. Whenever there was a question concerning the truth, there was no need and no room for debate. The question had to be brought to the Vatican. The pope and his archbishops would then study the issue and give a "holy decree," which was the final decision. Thus the Bible was closed for ten centuries, from the end of the sixth century until the completion of the Reformation at the end of the sixteenth century. In Western history this period, which lasted a full one thousand years, is called the

Dark Ages. Today, because of the influence of the Protestant churches, the Catholic church no longer controls the Bible as tightly as before, and many Catholics read the Bible. But the final interpretation of the truth is still decided for them by the pope.

AFTER THE REFORMATION

The purpose of my speaking concerning this is for you to know that before the Reformation led by Martin Luther, even during the time the Bible was locked up by the Roman Catholic church, there were still some raised up by the Lord to know the Bible. By this we see that there were three periods: from the apostles to the Council of Nicaea (325 A.D.), from the Council of Nicaea to about 590 A.D., and the centuries during which the Bible was locked up by the Catholic church. After the Reformation, the Bible under the Protestant churches was made public, being freed from the chains of Catholicism. However, very few had opened this book; it still remained closed. Today in the United States, for example, the book of Revelation is, for the most part, still a closed book. Nevertheless, after the time of Luther, people continued to study the Bible. They discovered not only justification by faith but also sanctification by faith. Out of this discovery came the holiness groups. In the 1690s Bible readers discovered that in the Bible baptism does not mean washing or sprinkling but "dipping into." The Greek word *baptizo* means "to dip into." From this discovery came the Baptists. At approximately the same time, Bible scholars also found that it is the elders who should oversee the church. They saw according to the Bible that it should not be as in the Catholic church where the pope is the highest bishop, with cardinals, archbishops, and bishops under him. This kind of organization came into being as a result of the influence of a church father named Ignatius. He considered a bishop to be different from an elder. To him, an elder's administration is local, whereas a bishop's administration is regional. Therefore, the bishop's office is higher than that of an elder, and he can rule over an elder. This was the root of a tragedy that is still spreading today. Not only the Catholics have bishops, but the Church of England also has bishops. Those who saw the biblical principle of the eldership concerning the church forsook the practice of having bishops and considered that in each locality there should only be elders. Thus they established Presbyterianism.

THE BRETHREN BEING RAISED UP

At that time a group of people in Europe received light from the Bible to see that there should be no rank among believers in the Lord. Therefore, they called each other brother. These brethren suffered a double persecution from both the Catholics and the Protestants. Later, Zinzendorf was raised up by the Lord in Bohemia, in southern Germany. He received those brothers from the north who were being persecuted. The main group came from Moravia and became known as the Moravian Brethren. Zinzendorf also saw from the Bible that all the brothers should gather together in one place for meeting and should also go out to preach the gospel. Therefore, they practiced the church life and lived a life of migration. The number of their migrations was great, especially from Europe to America. Today there are still churches of the Moravian Brethren in the United States.

John Wesley, George Whitefield, and the master hymn writer Charles Wesley—all contemporaries of Zinzendorf—were also gained by the Lord. In the 1820s the Lord suddenly raised up the Brethren in England. Their condition was very strong. Many of them were knighted and held important government positions, yet they were absolute toward God and totally forsook the world. The greatest and most powerful teacher among them was J.N. Darby. He was a minister of the Church of England before he was thirty years of age. After attending a home meeting of the Brethren, he was immediately caught. He became the most gifted Bible expositor and is called "the king of Bible exposition."

THE INFLUENCE OF THE INNER LIFE GROUP

One hundred years after Luther's Reformation, Protestantism became dead, just as in the epistle of the Lord Jesus to the church in Sardis: "You have a name that you are living, and you are dead" (Rev. 3:1). Around that time a group of people in the Catholic church who loved the Lord began to pursue the inner life. They are known in church history as the mystics. The leading ones among them were Fenelon, Thomas Campbell, Madame Guyon, who was most influential, and Brother Lawrence, who was a cook in the army. They had a deep knowledge concerning the inner life to such an extent that their writings could not be practiced by common people. After a period of time, a brother named William Law, who was a scholar from England, edited the books of the mystics. This allowed many people to benefit from them. After this, Andrew Murray further improved the writings of the mystics by using plain words to bring out the deep truth. His book *The Spirit of Christ* was his masterpiece. Fifty years ago Brother Nee and I had a conversation in which he mentioned this book and told me that he would pay the publishing costs for anyone who would translate it.

In the book *The Spirit of Christ,* chapter five is the most valuable. In this chapter, which speaks of the Spirit of the glorified Jesus, Andrew Murray pointed out that today the Holy Spirit is different from the Spirit of God in the Old Testament. The Spirit of God in the Old Testament only had God's element, not the human element. In the New Testament, within the Spirit of the glorified Jesus there is the spirit of man, the element of man. This chapter opened my eyes, and I began to see that today the Spirit in the New Testament is a compound Spirit. In the Old Testament the Holy Spirit was purely the Spirit of God, having only the divine element. In the New Testament the Spirit is called the Spirit of Jesus Christ (Phil. 1:19). He is called not only the Spirit of God (Rom. 8:9) but also the Spirit of Jesus (Acts 16:7) and the Spirit of Christ (Rom. 8:9); hence, the Spirit of Jesus Christ. Thus, He is the all-inclusive supply.

Later, I also was helped by the Brethren to know that the holy anointing oil in Exodus 30 was not merely oil but an ointment. There were five elements in this ointment. Olive oil was mingled with four different spices to become a compound ointment. After the compounding, the constitution of the ointment was no longer the same. Based on what the Brethren and Andrew Murray saw, I studied the elements and discovered that the four spices truly signify the human living, death, resurrection, and ascension of the Lord. Based on this, I boldly say that today the Spirit of God has become the Spirit of Jesus Christ, and that this Spirit is a compound Spirit. By this example we can see that the teaching of the inner life people and of the Brethren have given us much help.

After Andrew Murray there was Jessie Penn-Lewis. She was also of the inner life group. Many portions of *The Spiritual Man,* which was written by Brother Nee, are translations of her books. After Jessie Penn-Lewis came T. Austin-Sparks. He could also be counted among the inner life group. All the above-mentioned persons could be categorized as Bible scholars. Besides these, in the 1860s there was a couple in England named Smith. Mrs. Smith wrote a book called *The Christian's Secret of a Happy Life.* This couple started a conference in Keswick, which rapidly developed into the best among the Christian conferences in England. The speakers there included many Bible scholars.

THE LORD'S RECOVERY AMONG US

We can see that from the time of the Apostles, through the time of the Council of Nicaea, and continuing until the twentieth century, there have been Bible scholars in every generation. We thank the Lord that most of the light that they saw has been put into writing. Sixty or more years ago we were raised up by the Lord. The first leading one among us was Brother Watchman Nee. He set a very good pattern by having no bias. He knew the proper way to read, and even the more he knew how to select books. From 1923 to 1925, when he was just over twenty years old, he collected many prominent Christian writings and Christian masterpieces, about three thousand books. This collection included books of the church fathers, books about church history, books of Bible scholars, and biographies of famous Christians with many of their good messages. He read nearly all of them. Later, I came into the Lord's recovery and became his co-worker. I thank the Lord that from the beginning Brother Nee had a high regard for me. He often sat down and discussed with me the books he had read. My memory was able to retain all that he spoke to me. He brought out many good points from the Catholic church, from the Greek Orthodox church, and from many of the Protestant denominations. He even brought out the good points from the Pentecostal movement. Some of our hymns are from the Pentecostal movement. Hymn #551, "Hallelujah! Hallelujah! I have passed the riven veil," is one of them. Hymn #310, "Glorious Freedom! Wonderful Freedom!" is another. These are masterpieces of the Pentecostal movement.

When we were raised up by the Lord, we were all modern young men. Our thoughts were quite advanced, and we did not follow anything blindly. One day while we were studying in college the Lord gained us. We began to read the Bible diligently and to study Christianity. We laid everything down to serve the Lord. We realized that we could not develop our practice in isolation, and that we needed to broaden our view by reading others' writings. Therefore, we labored to collect and to study all of the prominent writings from the two thousand year history of Christianity. We were not biased. Using the Bible as our standard, we accepted whatever was according to the Bible and rejected whatever was not according to the Bible.

Today, our writings in the Life-study of the Bible are the fruit of this diligent study. All these Life-studies are Bible expositions which include the twenty-seven books of the New Testament and two books of the Old Testament, Genesis and Exodus. These have been written according to what we have inherited in the past sixty years, according to all the revelations seen by the saints in the past, the aggregate of their visions, and are presented before you.

THE TEACHING OF THE BRETHREN

I want to point out that in understanding the Word of God, the most difficult thing is to depend on the teaching received by the saints in the past. In the previous message I pointed out our need to learn from the early saints. First, we need to depend much on the teaching of the Brethren. Their teaching is the higher theology. Today, the United States has the best theology, and the two most orthodox seminaries are Dallas Theological Seminary in Texas and Moody Bible Institute. Their theology is mainly from the Brethren. Moody Bible Institute was founded by D.L. Moody. His gospel truth all originated with the Brethren. Dallas Theological Seminary mainly uses Scofield's *Reference Bible,* and ninety percent of Scofield's teaching came from the Brethren. Therefore, if you want to study theology, you must use the Brethren theology. In addition, you need to be familiar with and have a deep knowledge of the teachings of the inner life group. The Brethren theology is too literal and too objective; it needs to be balanced by the life line of the inner life people. The inner life group emphasizes the inner life, the reality, rather than the explanation of the letter of the Word.

You must also be familiar with what Calvin saw concerning the revelation of predestination. He asserted that God chose and predestinated us in eternity past to be saved once for all (Eph. 1:4-5). Although this revelation is correct, the Arminians oppose this view. They believe that even though our salvation is by God's grace, if we do not fulfill our responsibility after being saved, we will lose our salvation. Therefore, in their view salvation is not once for all; after being saved we still may perish. But if we repent, we can be saved again. This concept totally emphasizes man's responsibility, and it is therefore called the doctrine of human responsibility. Of these two schools, we accept the former totally, and reject the latter entirely. Then how can we resolve the dispute between these two schools? How can they be balanced? According to the history of theology, after Calvin and Arminius, another group of theologians emerged, beginning from Govett, then Panton, and then

Pember. Their school has formed a line concerning the truth of the kingdom in the New Testament. They saw that once a person is saved he will not perish forever (John 10:28). However, in order to encourage those who follow Him faithfully after salvation, God has set up a kingdom full of requirements to be their reward. If one is faithful, he will be rewarded (Matt. 24:45-47; 25:19-23). If one is not faithful, he will be punished and will lose the kingdom, but he himself will still be saved (Matt. 24:48-51; 25:24-30; 1 Cor. 3:10, 12-15). This is called the truth of the kingdom reward and punishment.

Now we must lay hold of these five points: depending much on the theology of the Brethren, knowing and becoming familiar with the school of the inner life people, receiving Calvin's revelation of God's predestination, rejecting the Arminian doctrine of human responsibility, and practicing the truth of the kingdom reward and punishment. I have told you all this even though you may not understand immediately. Later, when you—especially the young people—read the books among us, you will discover that what we say is similar to the Brethren theology and similar to the life line of the mystics, and that we also acknowledge absolutely Calvin's view of God's predestination. The problem pointed out by the Arminians is not concerning perdition but concerning being unable to receive the kingdom. Although the Bible does say that a saved person may still have problems, this refers to the punishment and loss during the kingdom age. All the verses in the Bible fall into place with these five points.

SOME IMPORTANT TRUTHS
THAT HAVE BEEN MISUNDERSTOOD

In this message we come to a very important subject, that is, some important truths that have been misunderstood. There are many Bible truths which have been misunderstood. In fact, not many today have learned the Bible in an orderly, orthodox, and step-by-step way. This was why in a previous message I showed you the way to understand the truth. We must understand it literally, and we also need to take care of the context, using the entire Bible to explain any one verse. Furthermore, we need to go beyond the letter to search for the revelation of life. Then we need to remember that the Brethren theology is the best and should be accepted. The things of the inner life school and Calvin's vision of God's predestination should also be accepted. But the Arminian doctrine of human responsibility should not be accepted. Furthermore, the truth of the kingdom reward and punishment also should be accepted. If these are kept in mind, our Bible exposition will be more or less up to the standard. After these messages are printed, I hope that everyone will have a copy. These messages should serve as an eternal reminder that the Bible should not be expounded loosely. By following these principles, our expounding of the Bible will not get off the track.

Today, five of the greatest Bible truths are being ignored and misunderstood by people: God's economy, God's dispensing, the divine Trinity, the God-Man Jesus, and the mingling of God and man. In this message we will consider the first two truths, and in the next message, the remaining three.

GOD'S ECONOMY

First, God's economy is God's household administration, arrangement, and plan. Even though the Chinese word for "economy" is old and perhaps not often used, it is nevertheless a good word. More than sixty years ago I heard people use the Chinese expression "to be full of economy." The meaning of this phrase is to be full of rules, plans, ideas, and arrangements. When we see the heavens and the earth created by God, we know that He is full of ability and accomplishments.

God has a big family; therefore, He has His household administration, which is His arrangement, or plan. According to the Bible, this is His economy. Ephesians 3:9-11 says, "And to bring to light what is the dispensation [economy] of the mystery, which from the ages has been hidden in God, who created all things; in order that now to the rulers and the authorities in the heavenlies might be made known through the church the multifarious wisdom of God, according to the purpose of the ages which He made in Christ Jesus our Lord." The purpose of the ages means the eternal purpose. Here we see that there is a mystery hidden in God. His mystery is to gain a church to express His wisdom. Therefore, this mystery of His became His arrangement, and His arrangement is both His economy and His plan. I can only say this much. Please go back and read carefully this portion of the Bible, which is very deep.

Ephesians 1:9-10 says, "Having made known to us the mystery of His will, according to His good pleasure which He purposed in Himself unto a dispensation [economy] of the fullness of the times, to head up all things in Christ, the things in the heavens and the things on the earth, in Him." Ephesians 3:9-11 says that God's economy is His mystery with the purpose of gaining a church. Ephesians 1:9-10 says, "Unto a dispensation [economy] of the fullness of the times, to head up all things in Christ." This heading up is through the church. We will see this condition when the New Jerusalem is manifested. The New Jerusalem is the church. Its center is Christ. Through the New Jerusalem God will head up all things in Christ that the glory of God may be expressed eternally. This is God's economy.

When young brothers and sisters are just beginning to read the Bible, they may feel that this point does not mean much. They should not say this, because this point will be a great help to them. Because many people do not know this point, their understanding of the Bible is not only superficial but also near-sighted. They do not have a broad or long-range view. Today many Christians only observe the doctrines found in the four Gospels and in part of the Acts. They do not go further. Therefore in their reading they do not see the church or the New Jerusalem, which comes after the church.

First, God's household administration is His household management. With the household management there is the administration. Paul was one who received the ministry from this household management; he even received the greatest ministry. He was a great steward in God's household management. He knew that the mystery of Christ is the church (Eph. 3:2-4), and as a steward he completed the Word of God, that is, the mystery which was hidden from the ages and from the generations. If Paul did not write his fourteen Epistles, the Word of God would not have been completed. The completed Word is a mystery, and this mystery is Christ as the hope of glory in the believers (Col. 1:25-27). Paul first understood that the mystery of Christ is the church; then he wrote down all that he had seen. Thus the divine revelation and the Word of God were completed. Finally, he preached the unsearchable riches of Christ to God's chosen people (Eph. 3:8). Thus, God's dispensing was produced.

GOD'S DISPENSING

Now we come to the second point—God's dispensing. Even though we cannot find the term dispensing in the New Testament, the fact is there. First, God's dispensing is the goal of God's economy, and, second, it is to dispense the unsearchable riches of Christ in the rich operation of the Triune God to us, the believers in Christ (Eph. 3:8). Today the riches of the Triune God are always moving and operating in order to dispense the unsearchable riches which have been stored up by Christ, little by little, to His believers. This is God's dispensing. Second Corinthians 13:14 says, "The grace of the Lord Jesus Christ, and the love of God, and the fellowship of the Holy Spirit be with you all." Grace is of Christ, love is of the Father, and fellowship is of the Spirit. Love is the source, grace is the manifestation and the flowing out, and fellowship is the transmission, the delivering. The flowing out of love is grace, the moving of grace is fellowship, and by the coming of the fellowship these things reach us. Hence, we receive love, we receive grace, and we also receive fellowship. This is the operation of the riches of the Triune God to infuse the unsearchable riches that have been stored in Christ into us. This dispensing is for the producing of the church (Eph. 3:10).

I want to say a word of warning here. Paul said in 1 Corinthians 3:17, "If anyone destroys the temple of God, God shall destroy him." Today we must be careful concerning our attitude towards the church. Whoever destroys the church of God will suffer loss. This is a serious matter, because God in His mystery has an economy, a plan to obtain a church. For this cause He even dispenses His riches in Christ to His chosen people, the believers in Christ, in order to produce a corporate expression. Therefore, the church is a pearl in the eyes of God. No one can hurt or damage her without suffering loss and even being destroyed by God.

THE RESULT OF GOD'S DISPENSING

Finally, the result of God's dispensing is the church becoming the fullness of Christ (Eph. 1:23). Remember, the fullness is the expression. This may be illustated by the water in a cup. If the cup is not full, the water cannot be manifested. But once the water overflows, it is manifested. The church being the fullness of Christ means that the church is the overflowing of Christ, that is, the expression of Christ. The result of being the expression of Christ is to be the fullness of God, that is, the expression of God. Praise the Lord! This is God's dispensing, which is produced out of the economy of God. These are two of the greatest truths in the Bible.

CHAPTER FIVE

SOME IMPORTANT ITEMS OF THE TRUTH THAT HAVE BEEN MISUNDERSTOOD

(2)

Scripture Reading: Matt. 28:19; Eph. 4:6; Heb. 1:8; Acts 5:3-4; Isa. 9:6; Heb. 1:12; 7:3; 9:14; John 14:10-11; 5:43; 14:26; 15:26; 6:46; 8:29; 10:30; Luke 1:35; Matt. 1:18, 20; John 16:14-15; 1 Cor. 15:45; 2 Cor. 3:17; Matt. 1:18, 20, 21, 23; Rom. 9:5; Col. 2:9; 1 Tim. 2:5; Acts 7:56; Rev. 1:13; Matt. 26:64; Rev. 14:14; John 1:51, 12-13; Rom. 11:24; John 6:48, 57; 7:37-39; 1 Cor. 6:17; Lev. 2:4

OUTLINE

III. Some important items of the truth that have been misunderstood:
  C. The divine Trinity—Matt. 28:19:
    1. The Father, the Son, and the Spirit all being God—the only one God—Eph. 4:6; Heb. 1:8; Acts 5:3-4.
    2. The Father, the Son, and the Spirit coexisting simultaneously from eternity to eternity—Isa. 9:6; Heb. 1:12; 7:3; 9:14.
    3. The Father, the Son, and the Spirit coinhering and being inseparable—John 14:10-11; 5:43; 14:26; 15:26.
    4. The Son coming with the Father, the Father being with the Son, and the Son and the Father being one—John 6:46; 8:29; 10:30.
    5. The Son being incarnated through the Spirit's conception and being filled with the Holy Spirit while living and moving in the flesh— Luke 1:35; Matt. 1:18, 20.
    6. All that the Father has being the Son's and

all that the Son possesses being received by
the Spirit—John 16:14-15.

7. The Son being called the Father and becoming
the Spirit—Isa. 9:6; 1 Cor. 15:45; 2 Cor. 3:17.

D. The God-man Jesus:

1. Conceived of the Holy Spirit, thus having the
divine element—Luke 1:35; Matt. 1:18, 20.

2. Born of a virgin, thus having the human
element—Matt. 1:21, 23.

3. Born as God and man—a God-man—being
the complete God (Rom. 9:5; Col. 2:9) and the
perfect man (1 Tim. 2:5)—Isa. 9:6, the child
being called the mighty God.

4. Still being the Son of Man after His resurrection and ascension into heaven—Acts 7:56;
Rev. 1:13.

5. Still being the Son of Man in His second
coming—Matt. 26:64; Rev. 14:14.

6. Being the Son of Man forever in eternity—
John 1:51.

E. The mingling of God and man:

1. In the Lord Jesus:

a. Conceived of the Holy Spirit in the womb
of the virgin Mary—the divine element
mingling with the human element, without
producing a third element—Matt. 1:18,
20-21, 23.

b. The Son of God born as the Son of Man—
the two becoming a God-man, without
producing a third person.

2. In the believers:

a. Being born of God to become children of
God—John 1:12-13—having the human element mingled with the divine element,
without producing a third element.

b. The branches of the wild olive tree being
grafted into the cultivated olive tree—Rom.
11:24—the two not only becoming one tree,
but the two lives also mingling together to

produce a compound fruit, not a fruit of a third nature.

c. The Lord being the bread of life for the believers to eat and the Holy Spirit being the living water for the believers to drink— John 6:48, 57; 7:37-39—the elements of what is eaten and drunk mingling and becoming one with the person who eats and drinks, thus becoming the element of the person who eats and drinks without producing a third element.

d. The believers being joined to the Lord and becoming one spirit—1 Cor. 6:17—the mingling of the spirit of the believer and the Spirit of the Lord to become one spirit.

e. The fine flour of the meal offering being mingled with oil to become the cake of the meal offering—Lev. 2:4—the mingling of two elements to become one substance without producing a third kind of element.

BEING CONCERNED
FOR THE FULL-TIME BROTHERS AND SISTERS

I am concerned about the more than two hundred full-timers who are here. I care for this matter very much because it is a matter of great importance to me. You have graduated from college; you are young and have a great future, yet you have given up everything to trust the Lord and learn to serve Him. This is of great value, even if there is only one full-timer, not to mention two hundred. Since there are two hundred of you, I feel that I have so much in my heart that I want to do, yet my strength is very limited. I would like to be with you all the time for ten years to do nothing else but study the Bible. I believe this would make my heart happy, and I would be satisfied. I would have two hundred disciples to study with me for ten years. This would be a tremendous thing.

However, after weighing the situation, I feel that I cannot let this work go. During these few days I have been tossing back and forth, even in my sleep at night. What is the reason? I visited Australia in April of 1971. At that time there were no churches in Australia, although there were several churches in New Zealand. It has been fourteen and a half years since my last visit, and now there are twelve churches that have been raised up in Australia. Recently, I received a letter from Australia saying, "Now is the time that you should come." Thus there is a turmoil in my heart. Although I would only spend a week in Australia, it would make a great difference here whether I go or not. Whether or not I can spare this one week depends on the work here. I really would like to stay here to do something with you two hundred full-timers. I also hope that the number of full-time brothers and sisters will increase to five hundred. Five hundred full-time brothers and sisters could be produced on the island of Taiwan each year. Because of the need for my going to Australia, I have to work harder.

In the previous messages I spoke on the way to know God's Word. You should have more fellowship on the points in those messages. They are all basic principles.

After that I continued to speak on the five major theological problems that were ignored and misunderstood throughout history. In the last message I gave you two major problems: God's economy and God's dispensing. I do not believe that you have thoroughly understood the previous message. But I hope that after this week is over, the young people, especially those brothers and sisters who are full-timers, will make an effort to study these two major problems. When you study, you need to search out all the books in the Gospel Book Room that are related to God's economy and God's dispensing. Study together to enter into these two very basic truths.

In this message I will give you three more topics. The first topic is the divine Trinity, that is, the Triune God. The second topic is the God-man Jesus. This topic is related to Christ's person, to what is called Christology in theology. The third topic is the mingling of God and man.

Ever since the passing away of the apostles, beginning from the second century, the questions of the Triune God and Christ's person have been the focal points of debates. These debates have continued even until today. Although there are many inaccuracies in these debates, some of the debaters are scholars who have had very deep insights. We can say that today we inherit what they have seen, and we stand on their shoulders. However, the Lord has been merciful to us and has enlightened us during these years. On the one hand we inherited something from them, and on the other hand we have been enlightened further. What I have given you in the outline of this message is a product of what we inherited and what we ourselves have seen. It is very simple and yet very accurate. You are still young, and you should not enter into these debates, because once you get into them you will find yourself in a maze that you cannot escape. I have passed through this. Therefore, based on what others have seen through the debates in the past, plus the light that we have received, I have written the crucial points in the outline.

THE DIVINE TRINITY

First let us consider the divine Trinity. The first time the Bible clearly speaks of the divine Trinity is in Matthew 28:19. In that verse the Lord commanded the disciples, saying, "Go therefore and disciple all the nations, baptizing them into the name of the Father and of the Son and of the Holy Spirit." This verse clearly mentions the Father, the Son, and the Spirit. Although the Triune God was revealed in the Old Testament, it was not until the Lord Jesus, who is God, passed through four crucial steps—incarnation, human living, crucifixion, and resurrection—that He spoke to His disciples before ascending to heaven, saying, "All authority has been given to Me in heaven and on earth. Go therefore and disciple all the nations, baptizing them into the name of the Father and of the Son and of the Holy Spirit" (Matt. 28:18-19). The name signifies the person. Hence, to baptize people into the name of the Father and of the Son and of the Holy Spirit is to baptize people into the Father, the Son, and the Holy Spirit. Thus, it was after His resurrection that the Lord Jesus clearly spoke of the Father, the Son, and the Holy Spirit, because before His resurrection, the Spirit of the Triune God—the Father, the Son, and the Spirit—was not yet completed. This is the reason John 7:39 says, "For the Spirit was not yet, because Jesus was not yet glorified." When was Jesus glorified? He was glorified in resurrection (Luke 24:26). Therefore, after His resurrection, the Spirit was completed.

THE HEAVENS, THE EARTH, AND ALL THINGS BEING FOR MAN

We must realize that God was our God in eternity past, before the existence of the heavens and the earth. He is God who is triune—the Father, the Son, and the Spirit. However, before the creation, this Triune God had not passed through any process; He was simply the eternal God. There was no human element in Him because man was not yet created. There was no human essence, and at that time there were no human beings living in the universe. He had not passed through the all-inclusive death and had not entered into resurrection. In eternity past, this Triune God was simply triune—the Father, the Son, and the Spirit. However, He had a plan; He wanted to dispense Himself into the men whom He had chosen. This is the focus, and this is His goal. However, where were the men whom He had chosen?

In order to have the men whom He had chosen as the object of His glorious work, He created the heavens and the earth and all things in the universe. Speaking from the view of the existence of mankind, the heavens are for the earth. If there is sunshine, rain, and air, the creatures on earth can exist. The earth is mainly for the creatures—the plants and animals. Then for whom are the plants and animals? They are for us. Medical doctors have told us that for our existence, we need plants, animals, and minerals. With the support of these three we can live. Through the working together of the sunshine, water, and air from the heavens and the plants, animals, and minerals from the earth, we can live.

THE TRIUNE GOD HAVING
PASSED THROUGH A PROCESS

After the creation of the heavens and the earth and all things in them, God created man. After the creation of man, God could come to dispense Himself into man. When God came, He came not in the person of the Father but in the person of the Son. Although He came in the person of the Son, it does not mean that the Father was left behind, but it means that the Father came in the Son. Furthermore, when the Son came, He came mingled with the Spirit. The Son became flesh with the Father in Him and also with the Spirit. Therefore, the Bible does not say that the Son became flesh, but it says that God became flesh (John 1:1, 14). The One who became flesh is the very Triune God, the complete God. In this way the process proceeded step by step.

The first step was that this eternal God completed the work of creation, and He Himself came into the man whom He had chosen. The second step was His living on the earth for thirty-three and a half years. In those thirty-three and a half years He simply lived a human life. He experienced all the human hardships, sufferings, temptations, trials, and persecutions. In this process He manifested that He was the complete God and the perfect man. As God, He had no lack—the Father, the Son, and the Spirit were all included in Him. As man, He had no shortage—He was absolutely perfect. He was such a One, both God and man, the mysterious God-man. Therefore, He was qualified to accomplish the third step, that is, to die on the cross. Furthermore, He died with seven statuses: first, the Lamb of God (John 1:29); second, a man in the flesh (John 1:14; Rom. 8:3); third, the brass serpent (John 3:14); fourth, the last Adam (1 Cor. 15:45; Rom. 6:6); fifth, the Firstborn of all creation (Col. 1:15); sixth, the Peacemaker (Eph. 2:14-16); and seventh, the grain of wheat (John 12:24). The first six items dealt with the negative things to eliminate the things that should not have been there. The last item, on the positive side, released the divine life that we may receive life. Now He has passed through the all-inclusive death to clear away all the negative things, including sin—our sinful nature—the sins which we committed, Satan, the satanic world, the flesh, the old man, the old creation, and the divisions, the ordinances, and the habits among human beings. Like a great broom, His death swept away all the negative things in the universe. He was also the divine grain of wheat who through death released the divine life within Him.

The fourth step was that He resurrected. Through resurrection His body entered into glory and He became the life-giving Spirit. In this we can see that this life-giving Spirit is the ultimate consummation of the processed Triune God, who passed through incarnation, human living, death, and resurrection. At this point the Triune God is not merely God; in Him is the human nature, the human element, the human living, the effectiveness of His all-inclusive death, and the element of His resurrection. Now this rich Triune God is consummated as the life-giving Spirit. This life-giving Spirit is the Lord Jesus today. The Lord is the Spirit (2 Cor. 3:17). The Spirit was not yet before His resurrection (John 7:39), but the Spirit was there after His resurrection. What we mean by "was there" is that the Spirit is the ultimate consummation of the processed Triune God. Now, when we call upon the name of the Lord, the Spirit comes into us to be received by us. In speaking, this is very deep, but it is very simple in our experience. This is the way the Triune God is dispensed into us. We first need to grasp this point.

THE TRUTH OF THE DIVINE TRINITY

Now let us consider the first point on the outline—the divine Trinity.

The Father, the Son, and the Spirit All Being God—the Only God

Ephesians 4:6 says that the Father is God; Hebrews 1:8 says that the Son is God; and Acts 5:3-4 says that the Spirit is God.

The Father, the Son, and the Spirit Coexisting Simultaneously from Eternity to Eternity

Isaiah 9:6 says that the Father is the everlasting Father. Hebrews 1:12 says that the Son is eternal, that His years shall not fail, and Hebrews 7:3 says that He has no beginning of days nor end of life. Hebrews 9:14 says that the Spirit is the eternal Spirit. We can see that all Three— the Father, the Son, and the Spirit—coexist simultaneously without succession from eternity to eternity.

The Father, the Son, and the Spirit Coinhering and Being Inseparable

John 14:10-11 says that the Son is in the Father and the Father is in the Son; They coinhere. Most Christians believe that when the Son, the Lord Jesus, came to the earth, He left the Father in heaven. This is a wrong concept.

We need to realize that when the Lord Jesus was on earth, He was still in the Father and the Father was in

Him. John 5:43 says that the Lord Jesus came in the name of the Father. This means that He was in the Father. When He came, the Father came, because He was in the Father and the Father was in Him. John 14:26 says, "But the Comforter, the Holy Spirit, whom the Father will send in My name, He will teach you all things, and remind you of all things which I said to you." First, all Three of the Triune God—"the Comforter" (the Holy Spirit), "the Father," and "I" (the Son)—are mentioned in this verse. The Lord said, "The Holy Spirit, whom the Father will send in My name." This word means that the Father sends the Holy Spirit in the name of the Lord. That is to say, the Spirit, the sent One, is in the name of the Son. The result is that the Sender is in the Son and the sent One is also in the Son.

Isaiah 9:6 says that the name of the Son given to us is the "everlasting Father." Second Corinthians 3:17 also says, "And the Lord is the Spirit." Hence, the Son is the Father, and the Son is also the Spirit. It is impossible to separate the mystery of the Trinity. Let us look again at John 15:26: "But when the Comforter comes, whom I will send to you from the Father, the Spirit of reality who proceeds from the Father." Here the meaning of the Greek word translated "from" is "from with." The Son sends the Spirit and the Spirit comes "from" the Father and "with" the Father. The result is that the Spirit comes with the Father. But John 6:46 says, "Not that anyone has seen the Father, except Him who is from God, He has seen the Father." The word "from" here in Greek also has the sense of "from with." Thus, when the Son came, He came also with the Father.

The Father, the Son, and the Spirit
All Coming Together

When we look at John 6:46 and 15:26 together, we realize that the Father, the Son, and the Spirit all come together. John 6:46 says that the Son comes with the Father, and John 15:26 says that the Son sends the Spirit from the Father, and the Spirit comes with the Father.

Apparently, when the Spirit came, the Son was left in heaven. But John 6:46 says that the Son comes from the Father and with the Father, and John 14:26 says that the Father sends the Spirit in the Son. Therefore, putting these three verses together, we see that the Father, the Son, and the Spirit all come. Apparently when the Lord Jesus came to the earth, He was only the Son of God who became flesh, but actually, the Father was in Him and the Spirit was also in Him. He came in the name of the Father, and the Spirit also came in His name. Simply speaking, when He came, all Three—the Father, the Son, and the Spirit— came. Because He is the Triune God, the Three are inseparable.

For this reason, I feel that I must labor to show you such a simple outline together with the solid proof of the Scripture verses. We have studied the Bible for decades and have emphasized this point very much. This truth is very important. What Christianity preaches is too simplified, too traditional, and it is just hearsay. We have labored much to find out all the details. We discovered that the coming of the Lord Jesus is not so simple. It is not like the preaching of Christianity, which says that the Father and the Son are separate Persons, that the Son came and the Father remained in the heavens, and that the Son and the Spirit are also separate Persons. Now we realize that when the Son comes, He comes with the Father. The Father is in Him, and He is joined to the Spirit. Also, the Spirit comes with the Father and in the Son. Therefore, the Three are one. The Father, the Son, and the Spirit coinhere and are inseparable.

We may briefly reiterate points 4 through 7 on the outline at the beginning of the message as follows: The Son comes with the Father, the Father is with the Son, and the Son and the Father are one (John 6:46; 8:29; 10:30). The Father has never left the Son; He is always with the Son. Furthermore, the Son became flesh through the conceiving of the Spirit, and the Son was filled with the Holy Spirit in His living and moving in the flesh (Luke 1:35; Matt. 1:18, 20). All that the Father has belongs to the Son and all that the Son possesses is received by the Spirit (John 16:14-15). Finally, the Son is called the Father and also became the Spirit (Isa. 9:6; 1 Cor. 15:45; 2 Cor. 3:17). Eventually, the Father, the Son, and the Spirit all consummate in the Spirit. The Spirit is the ultimate consummation of the Triune God.

Modalism and Tritheism

Throughout history there have been two great heresies in the teaching of the Trinity. One is called modalism, which speaks of the Father, the Son, and the Spirit as follows: In the beginning God was the Father, and afterwards He became the Son. When He became the Son, the Father ceased to exist. Then the Son became the Spirit. When the Son became the Spirit, the Son also ceased to exist, and there was only the Spirit. Thus there is only one God with three modes; the Three—the Father, the Son, and the Spirit—do not exist simultaneously, but rather in succession. This is heresy. According to the modalistic view, first there was the Father, then there was the Son, and finally there is the Spirit. However, modalism has gone to the extreme in emphasizing one aspect of the truth—that God is uniquely one—and not being balanced by another aspect of the truth—that God is also three-in-one.

The other great heresy is tritheism, which says that the Father, the Son, and the Spirit coexist simultaneously and separately. The tritheists ignore the coinherence of the Father, the Son, and the Spirit. Thus, they separate the Triune God into three Gods. This is a prevailing heresy today. Many dare not confess that they hold this view because the Bible clearly says that there is only one God, but they believe this in their heart. Fifty years ago Wong Ming-Dao, a famous Chinese preacher, spoke strongly that the Father is a God, the Son is a God, and the Spirit is a God; thus, there are three Gods. A great opposition rose up because of this, and he gradually stopped preaching in this way, but inwardly he still believes this. Today, there are many preachers who also believe this.

According to my observation, in the United States many people believe that the Father, the Son, and the Spirit are three Gods. Furthermore, they do not think that there is anything wrong with this. To substantiate their belief some refer to the incident in Matthew 3:16-17, saying that when the Lord Jesus came up from His baptism and stood in the water, the Father spoke from heaven. They also point out that in John 17:1 the Lord lifted up His eyes to heaven and prayed, "Father... glorify Your Son that the Son may glorify You." They say that in this incident there are two Gods: one was praying and the other was listening to the prayer. It is clear that these people ignore the aspect that God is uniquely one and go to the extreme of emphasizing that God is three. This is also heresy. We have seen that the heresy of modalism says that the Father, the Son, and the Spirit exist in succession, and that eventually only one—the Spirit—is left. On the other hand, the heresy of tritheism speaks of the Father, the Son, and the Spirit coexisting simultaneously and thus being separate from each other, that is, being three from the beginning to the end.

The Essential Trinity and the Economical Trinity

The revelation in the Bible concerning this matter is between the two extremes of modalism and tritheism. We follow the Bible in taking such a stand. We bring the two extremes to the middle. We do not merely believe the aspect of God being uniquely one, nor do we merely believe the aspect of God being three. We believe that God is three-one, that is, that He is triune. This is a mystery.

In recent years, fifty young brothers and sisters in the United States have been collecting materials from the ancient writings. I have also collected many writings from the church fathers. Occasionally I refer to them and they have been helpful to me. The early fathers saw that there are two aspects of the divine Trinity: one is the aspect of essence, and the other is the aspect of economy. I fully understand what they meant.

Therefore, I spoke this clearly when I gave messages on

the Gospel of Luke and on God's New Testament economy (see *Life-study of Luke*, Message Fifty-two, and *God's New Testament Economy*, Chapters Twenty and Twenty-one). I spoke of the Trinity in two aspects: essential and economical. Speaking of God's existence, the Father, the Son, and the Spirit are inseparable and coexist simultaneously. But speaking of His plan, work, and move, first there is the Father, then the Son, and finally the Spirit. They are not simultaneous but in succession. In eternity past the Father planned; in the Gospels the Son accomplished what the Father planned; and in the Epistles the Spirit carries out what the Lord accomplished. The existence of the Triune God is essential, and His move is economical. Although this is the case, there is still the matter of His essence in His economical move.

The Holy Spirit came in the Lord Jesus' incarnation. Essentially, the Lord Jesus was conceived of the Holy Spirit, who is the essence of God, and this conception was a mingling of the divine element with the human element. Therefore, when the Lord Jesus was born, although He was a child, His name was the mighty God (Isa. 9:6). When the Lord Jesus was baptized at the age of thirty, He stood in the water and the Holy Spirit descended upon Him (Matt. 3:16-17). This was different from His birth. He was conceived of the Holy Spirit and born of a virgin. At that time the Holy Spirit was already in Him as His essence and element. But when He came up from the water, the Holy Spirit descended from heaven. This is the economical aspect. During the thirty-three and a half years while the Lord Jesus was on the earth, until His death the Holy Spirit was in Him. That is, God was in Him and with Him. He Himself said that the Father never left Him when He was on the earth (John 8:29). This is the essential aspect. But when He was crucified on the cross, He cried, "My God, My God, why have You forsaken Me?" (Matt. 27:46). We need to realize that this forsaking was not essential but economical. Essentially, the death of the Lord Jesus on the cross was the death of a God-man. But economically, God left Him. Then after His resurrection, He breathed the life-giving Spirit into His disciples (John 20:22) and He poured out the Spirit upon them on the day of Pentecost (Acts 2:1-4, 14-18, 33). Essentially, the Holy Spirit was breathed into them for their existence, and economically, He was poured upon them for their work.

THE GOD-MAN JESUS

Now we come to the fourth point—the God-man Jesus. As a God-man, the Lord Jesus was conceived of the Holy Spirit, thus having the divine element (Luke 1:35; Matt. 1:18, 20). He was also born of a virgin, thus having the human element (Matt. 1:21, 23). He was born as God and man—a God-man. He is the complete God (Rom. 9:5; Col. 2:9) and the perfect man (1 Tim. 2:5). In Isaiah 9:6 the child is called the mighty God. The child is human and the mighty God is God. Thus, He is God, yet also man.

Furthermore, even after His resurrection and ascension into heaven He is still the Son of Man (Acts 7:56; Rev. 1:13). Many Christians have the concept that the Lord Jesus became a man in His incarnation, but that He was no longer a man after His resurrection. In other words, they think that He put off His humanity. But in Acts 7:56 it is recorded that when Stephen was persecuted and martyred, he saw the Son of Man, Jesus, standing at the right hand of God. Also, when the Lord Jesus was judged on earth, He responded to the questions of the high priest by saying, "You shall see the Son of Man sitting at the right hand of power and coming on the clouds of heaven" (Matt. 26:64). Therefore, in His second coming He will still be a man. For eternity, He will still be the Son of Man. In John 1:51 the Lord said, "You shall see heaven opened and the angels of God ascending and descending on the Son of Man." This verse speaks of eternity future. The Lord still has flesh and bones after His resurrection (Luke 24:39). He is God and also man. What a mystery, and how glorious! In eternity past, He was God and not man. But after His incarnation, He is God and also man. He is not part of God, but the complete Triune God. He is the Father, the Son, and the Spirit. He is also a perfect man. Therefore He is a God-man.

THE MINGLING OF GOD AND MAN
In the Lord Jesus

Now let us consider the mingling of God and man. This is also one of the items for which we have been condemned strongly by some. The Bible clearly records that the Lord Jesus was conceived of the Holy Spirit in the womb of the virgin Mary. Conception is a matter of mingling. An ordinary conception is the mingling of a male and a female. The conception of the Lord Jesus is the mingling into one of God's element with the human element. Such a mingling can never produce a third kind of element. The slanderers say that I preach that Christ is neither a man nor God, but that He is of a third nature. Actually, I said that the divine element mingles with the human element and does not produce a third element. The Son of God was born to be the Son of Man. The two became a God-man, being God and also being man. This did not produce a third person.

In the Believers

First, the believers are born of God to become children of God (John 1:12-13). In such a birth the human element mingles with the divine element as one but does not produce a third element. Today, we are children of God. We are not adopted; we are born of God.

Second, the believers, as branches of the wild olive tree, were grafted into the cultivated olive tree (Rom. 11:24). The two have not only become one tree but are also mingled into one life to produce a compound fruit, not a fruit of a third nature. Our opposers say that our attachment to the Lord Jesus is a matter of being joined, and that it is not a mingling. On the contrary, I must say that the grafting of the branches of the wild olive tree into the cultivated olive tree is not only a joining outwardly, but even more it is a mingling of the inward life. Grafting is a mingling; two lives are mingled into one to produce a compound fruit, not a fruit of a third nature.

Third, the Lord is the bread of life for the believers to

eat, and the Holy Spirit is the living water for the believers to drink (John 7:37-39). The element of the food mingles and becomes one with the person who eats, becoming the element of the person who eats without producing a third element. Is it not ridiculous to say that the food which we eat is only joined with us and is not mingled with us? When we drink water, surely the water mingles with us. Those who oppose us cannot receive the concept of mingling because they are influenced by tradition. They say, "What? Mingle with God? Then do you become God, and does God become you?" My answer is this: "If God is still God and I am still I, then I have not been saved yet! What I mean when I say that I become one with God is only that I have God's life, nature, and image, but I do not have the position to be worshipped by men."

It is obvious that the son of a king has the life and nature of the king, but he is not the king and does not have the position of the king. We are children born of God, and we have the life and nature of God. It is clearly stated in 1 John 3:2 that "if He is manifested, we shall be like Him." Paul also clearly says, "It is no longer I who live, but Christ lives in me" (Gal. 2:20). He also said, "For to me to live is Christ" (Phil. 1:21). In a few hours, the food that we eat is digested and assimilated to become our cells, blood, bones, and flesh. We are constituted of what we eat.

Fourth, the believers are joined to the Lord and have become one spirit with Him (1 Cor. 6:17). This is the mingling of the believer's spirit and the Spirit of the Lord to become one spirit—the mingling of God and man.

Fifth, in the mingling of the fine flour with oil to become the cake in the meal offering (Lev. 2:4), two elements are mingled to become one substance. They do not produce a substance with a third kind of element. The oil is mingled with the flour. Flour signifies humanity and oil signifies God. This also speaks of the mingling of God and man.

LEARNING TO USE THE TRUTHS,
WHICH ARE TODAY'S MODERN WEAPONS

I have presented these truths to you. You must study diligently and do much research; then you will know the five major truths: God's economy, God's dispensing, the divine Trinity, the God-man Jesus, and the mingling of God and man. These are the five basic truths in the Bible. Our vision is based on these five truths. Although the opposition in the United States has been somewhat subdued, these waves of theological debates will still flow to Taiwan. Sooner or later, you will meet others saying that your Brother Lee teaches heresy on matters such as the Trinity, dispensing, mingling, and the God-man. I am afraid that if you do not have a good foundation now, when the time comes you will not have the words to respond. This is why I have pointed out these verses to you now. When these matters come up for discussion, you can bring out these verses and read them to the opposers one by one. They will have no ground for debate after they have seen these verses because the truth is the truth.

I have used the simplest method to present to you these deep things. I hope you will exercise to be equipped. Study the truths. They are our modern weapons.